The Serious Consequences of Economic Woes

Adam Paine, PhD

Copyright © 2021 by Adam Paine

All rights reserved. No part of this publication may be reproduced, stored in a retrieval system, or transmitted in any form or by any means, electronic, mechanical, photocopying, recording or otherwise, without the prior permission of the publishers.

Preface

This book introduces various practical topics relating to the economy. The economy has always been hard to manage, frequently resulting in recessions, retrenchments, unemployment and other hardships. There are many suggestions for handling economic problems and averting economic crises in the book, including some suggestions on curbing the ills of capitalism.

It is one of the most important books, if not the most important, that I have written.

Adam Paine, PhD
August 5, 2021

Contents

1	The Problems of Economic Downturn	5
2	Keynes' Ideas	7
3	Changes in Economic Affairs	8
4	Greed in Practice	12
5	Technological Changes	14
6	Small Industries	18
7	World Recession and Possible Remedies	23
8	Changing Jobs and Skill and Talent Distribution	24
9	Some Possible Solutions to Economic Problems	25
10	More Possible Solutions to Economic Problems	28
11	Economic Problems, Capitalism and Possible Solutions	32
12	Covid-19 Pandemic, the Economy and Possible Remedies	47
	Reading List	50

1

The Problems of Economic Downturn

The last economic downturn had occurred many years ago, whence, the author now recalls, there had been endemic retrenchment exercises by corporations. Keynes, the brilliant British economist, had held that the economy, if left to itself without government intervention, tended to end up with more problems, whilst his predecessors, the so-called Classical economists, had held the belief that the economy, if left alone, would always right itself or overcome all its problems; he had advocated governmental role in steering the economy smoothly, e.g., through expenditure on public works and fiscal measures. Keynes has been proven right now and again in having believed that the economy tends to go awry if left alone, as even with government intervention the economy still often goes wrong.

We know that it is not easy to get the economy going smoothly. Has not the USA, e.g., been having world-class economists such as Samuelson, Klein and Friedman to offer it and the rest of the world excellent economic advice at the Council of Economic Advisers and why has it been languishing from budget deficits, unemployment and inflation (in fact, the USA had experienced very bad budget deficits in the past)? The influence of Lord Keynes' ideas had been paramount too in the USA during the late President Franklin Roosevelt's time, when the New Deal had been formulated with Keynes' guiding hand.

We may ask ourselves here, "Why is the economy all the time troubled by inflation, unemployment and the like?" We have made tremendous advances in science and technology, and yet we are no nearer to curing our economic ills. There had often been a great deal of publicity in the press about workers losing their jobs through redundancy - the marine industry in the author's country had been the first to be hit by the world recession, having "hit rock-bottom" many years ago - a few years later saw the going down of the electronics and building construction industries. Some electronic manufacturing companies had reduced their working week (e.g., from five working-days to four working-days), some had retrenched, some had closed down, with the other industries similarly affected. Many architectural firms and consultancies had also reduced their working week or retrenched staff, some had even resorted to reducing the pay of their staff to keep up with the hard time. Building contractors complained of shortage of contracts and contracts at "rock-bottom" prices. Developers adopted the "wait and see" attitude and were much more cautious in their investments. Even departmental stores and emporiums were not spared this painful fate - the mammoth Emporium Holdings Group in the author's country had then carried out a small retrenchment exercise, and that, after the staff had pledged loyalty to the management at an elaborate company gathering. The situation was bleak. We valued our jobs and feared losing them; many of our friends, neighbours and fellow citizens were out of work or were in new jobs at lower salaries.

How did all this affect us? Of course, the unemployed were likely to feel frustrated and worried. The employed also seemed worried about their future - who knew when the axe was going to fall? Everyone seemed more cautious about spending. When money did not change hands fast enough in the economy, business would not be viable. Businessmen were also more hesitant in their ventures; staff who had resigned might not be likely to be replaced; spending on new equipment and/or expansion programs were also likely to be held back. All these people who were affected by the economy would in turn affect the economy.

At this point, Keynes, if he were living today, might have urged governments to spend more on public works, create more jobs, or reduce taxes, to increase purchasing power and consumer demand, to prop up the economy. Had not the USA been doing that for years, so much so that it once faced the worst budget deficit in its history? Keynes' ideas did not seem to have worked well in the USA. Had they worked well elsewhere? Were they likely to work well at all, at least in some places? Our time is different from that of Keynes and may require a different set of solutions.

There seems then to have been too much adverse publicity from all quarters, especially the press, and this does not seem to have helped the economy in any way. Government leaders and other opinion leaders might have been unconsciously "dooming" the very people they hoped to bring salvation to by painting too many "dooms-day" pictures for them. This made everyone neurotic and pessimistic. This killed business adventurism, business enterprise, as businessmen over-reacted in response to all this.

Some years ago, there had been a great deal of publicity in the author's country about the booming building industry - the press talked about it, everybody spoke about it. The result - many people set up building-supplies companies (the author himself had been approached to help set up a building product manufacturing company) - many building construction foremen and managers gave up their secure jobs to set up their own building construction companies. A few years later they were caught by the economic downturn that more or less took everybody by storm.

It was all psychological. If, e.g., there were rumours, even unfounded rumours, that a certain bank was financially tottering, would not every account-holder of that bank rush to withdraw their savings out of fear? This analogy is aptly applicable to the economy.

Publicity and opinions of an adverse nature should thus be carefully regulated to prevent or minimise repercussions in the economy. Prophets of doom, pessimists and, generally, people with loud mouths or rumour-mongers of a perverse kind, should not be allowed to influence our opinions and attitudes to the detriment of the economy, of the people in general. How susceptible people often were. Just a few remarks from the US President, and speculators might become wildly excited and jump to conclusions; his views, his policies, carry much weight and have a great impact on business, especially business of a speculative nature such as the share market. Keynesian theories may work up to a certain degree, but the author feels that they ought to be reinforced by a government conducted program of publicity or propaganda to maintain, boost, or enhance business confidence or confidence in the economy. On the other hand, the mass media should be persuaded or restrained from painting too many bleak pictures of the economy, if the state of the economy is not to be worsened by declining public confidence.

Overstatement of the economic conditions could be greatly damaging. Calm and optimism should prevail, and the government should play its role well, if the business enterprise is not to be disintegrated.

2

Keynes' Ideas

John Maynard Keynes was a brilliant economist of the thirties. His ideas revolutionised economics. He brought an about-turn in the conception of politicians and economists regarding the economy. Starting from Jean Baptiste Say, brilliant French economist, the concept of economists thenceforth was that the economy tends towards full employment and equilibrium in market conditions. Keynes was to theoretise and prove that this was not the case. His many predictions about the British economy turned out to be true. Ironically, his theories were being practised by Hitler, consciously or unconsciously, and the result was just what Keynes predicted - full employment and high productivity in Nazi Germany. Perhaps, it was not a fair comparison, for Hitler was mesmeric and was able to rouse the people to heights of frenzy and was in effect a great motivator of man.

Unconscious to many, economics is the brother of politics, that is why it has been called "political economy". It is actually quite simple if politicians have that much power over the masses as Hitler had, in applying Keynes' theories. Keynes' theories would have brought thorough success everywhere. But his ideas were good only for his time and not for all times, and modifications here and there are necessary. The author would say that in order for Keynes' ideas to work, its advocate has to have the trust of and influence on the people. What is the use of providing ample employment so that full employment can be achieved when your people rather live on the dole than work? What is the point of pressing for higher productivity, when trade unions can dictate terms and twist arms, and workers are more interested in strikes than work?

A lot depends on the political skills of a country's leaders if all the factors of production, especially the variable factor of labour, are to be efficiently and effectively mobilised. People have to be moved towards achieving the ultimate desired goals by their leaders.

Contrariwise, if the people oppose the government more than they are being politically moved, much would be lost.

3

Changes in Economic Affairs

The times of Adam Smith, Thomas Malthus, David Ricardo and Karl Marx saw the landlord class and the peasant-working class in opposition (class struggle).

Then the early nineties saw the problems of unemployment and depression.

Now, the culprit is inflation, which worsens chronically into stagflation, whereby inflation and vast unemployment create disaster in the economy.

This is evolution of political economy in a nutshell. What must economics deal with in the very first place, if it claims to be a science that is capable of solving problems? Jeremy Bentham and his disciple John Stuart Mill thought that economics must be concerned with the "greatest happiness for the greatest number of people". The author is sure everyone must agree with them that economics must be concerned with this principle.

But this is quite often not the case. Capitalism may benefit only the few very rich people at the expense of the poorer ones, who are but "slaves" to their wealth-owning masters. Even governments have to respond to their beck and call at times because of the power over the economy they possess. When business flourishes, they recruit workers from all corners of the world if they could, if they are not available at home. When there is a recession, they will try to throw as much out as possible, jeopardising the livelihoods of wholly dependent families of the unemployed. Their control over the lives of their employees, they can make or break them, is almost absolute. They do not have to threaten you or manhandle you. But they can starve you by simply plucking you out of their payrolls.

It is strange that a long line of economists from Adam Smith to John Maynard Keynes, to Milton Friedman and Paul Samuelson, who have worked hard at solving the problems of economic survival, have hardly solved the world's economic problems. It appears like a case of a problem solved and a new problem cropping up. In the last analysis, it is the people who create their own problems and people are so unpredictable. The US has redoubtable economists like Samuelson and Friedman and yet its economy has been tottering. Where is the importance of fine economists and their theories? Economists may act as policy advisers to governments and rulers but governments and ministers need not act on their advice and would only promise and carry out what is politically expedient.

The society at large is getting more and more complex, of course, and with it too goes the economic problems. Capitalists and entrepreneurs are now faced with very demanding consumers. Now consumers try to go for excellence in styles of living. They simply refuse to watch black and white televisions and must enjoy the psychedelic delights of colour on televisions. Cars must come in style and modern designs. Clothes must be stylish and fit well. They want to buy things that are cheap but good in quality. They are very much more selective in consumption. They force factories and companies to close down by simply not buying their produce, which in turn leads to vast unemployment and great social problems. This in turn would adversely affect the consumers who are responsible for forcing the companies to close down. The cycle is a vicious one.

There is so much in the world to be done. Yet, so much talent, so much energy, is not made use of, and so many people have to go unemployed! If only corporations and government provide meaningful employment to these people, employment that brings satisfaction to not only the employee but to members of society. For example, unemployed people could be employed to do social work by the government, such as caring for and looking after the aged or the sick. Yet, their services are wasted and they are allowed to idle around and to turn delinquent even. Often when such people offer their services and their skills, their potential employers turn them down. Human beings seem to be such that if they cannot build they have to destroy; they cannot be expected to sit still and watch things go by.

Basically, capitalism hinges around the profit motive. Bosses employ workers who are expected to make a profit for them, otherwise they are of no bloody use. Bosses are often so demanding on their workers that they resort to exploitation. You may ask, "Where is the ethics of everything that your employer generally does?" Employers may argue that if they do not demand so much of their workers, their workers would perform at their minimal and their companies surely could not survive then. Little do they realise that the more they press their workers the more their workers are going to resist them. If their workers are courageous and active, they could organise industrial action such as go-slow or strike, and if they are the more passive type, they would simply not put in their best. But, on the other hand, if workers are made to feel that they belong to the company, they would automatically put in their best and be proud and happy of doing so. But workers have seldom been given such respect and good treatment and inevitably productivity is always a problem with many companies whose managers have never learnt to treat human beings as human beings. The profit motive is thus evil when it makes so many human beings, the workers, unhappy, and this unhappiness would inevitably spill over to members of the workers' families.

The whole concept of entrepreneurship and capitalism is egocentric, and, hence social problems are always inherent when there is egocentricity. Entrepreneurs claim to be desirous of bettering the lot of society through their services or products, whatever they are, quite often. But if you examine their deepest motive, you are likely to detect the self-centred aim of achieving wealth and power for the self. In all fairness to entrepreneurs, who could be regarded as the key people in a buoyant economy, it would be appropriate here to mention that the profit motive is definitely a spur for them to take the risk of business enterprise, but certainly they could be educated to adopt a more humane and caring attitude towards the society whom they are supposed to serve. The marketing concept whereby the consumer is regarded as "king" must be the uppermost in their mind and heart, upon whose patronisation they depend for survival. But often when a wealthy person is firmly established in his business, his head is high in the air, and the consumer becomes "nothing" and he could "take it or leave it".

In the past, the serfs were the working-class, and the lords and nobles were the employers. Today, we have supposedly become more civilised and humane, we have supposedly ridded ourselves of feudalism, which is by all account oppressive, little realising that in our new economic order, a neo-feudalism has already arisen. Only because people who influence our lives greatly benefit from this neo-feudalism, they "pretend" to us of the non-existence of or pretend to be ignorant of the existence of this neo-feudalism. Employers through their powers of dismissal of workers could be just as oppressive as feudal tyrants, but today educated people seem to take such things for granted. Only the trade unions take some stand over this question of employers' authority and rights. And in some countries, even the trade unions are suppressed. How does the working class protect themselves against being oppressed then? Sociologists may argue for the benefit of hierarchy in society but this hierarchy tends to be problem-ridden due to lack of trust and suspicion between the worker and his employer. In actuality, many employers of workers believe or feel that workers would not put in their best if not pushed or instilled with fear. This principle, I sincerely believe, is wrong. For basically, humanity treasures the feeling of freedom and the ability to use their initiative. The wars for independence, revolutions and what-not, were fought for the sake of this precious freedom from oppression. Surely, these fighters did not expect new shackles on their descendants, surely, the oppression the wealthy and the powerful exercise over their underlings is but a reverting to the oppressionism of the feudal past.

Economics, in all common sense, should be concerned with the "greatest happiness for the greatest number", but in practice it is actually the "greatest happiness for the smallest number", at least, the economy tends towards the latter. For example, a business competitor to obtain maximum profit for himself would tend to preclude other competitors by such means as price undercutting and so on; similarly employees in competing amongst themselves for jobs tend to bring down wage rates. They say in business jargon that the big fishes swallow the smaller fishes. Trade barriers, closed-shop policies, and the like, aim to bring less happiness and hope to certain people so that they give up their attempts in their business and advancement endeavours.

In today's economic order, where competition is very keen, the survival of a company, an organisation, or even, a whole nation, depends on productivity, a very vague term, albeit a somewhat technical one. Economists speak of supply-side economics, in the United States of America, for example. Here in the author's country, the government and everybody in business emphasise productivity. What exactly is productivity? It could mean many things to many people. Nevertheless productivity is the key to today's economic survival. Even if John Maynard Keynes, Adam Smith, Thomas Malthus, and the like, were living today, they would, in all likelihood, be recommending productivity. Productivity, for example, could be buying the cheapest raw materials and employing the cheapest labour. It could also mean the high motivation of the work-force which results in higher output. It could mean minimal input and maximum output. It could be incurring the lowest possible cost of production. It could be the greatest possible profit for the employer through tactical pricing. It could mean the introduction of better methods of production or automation. It could be the reduction of labour. It could be re-organisation. But in simple, basic terms, it means the best possible profit for the entrepreneur, i.e., it is up to the entrepreneur to decide whether he should maximise his profits at the expense of his workers, i.e., he resorts to exploitation, an unpleasant term to workers, or he should seek other means of maximising his profits without antagonising the workers. But more often than not, the workers would have to suffer because their employers want more profits or wish to retain their profits.

In actual fact, all workers would want to be treated fairly and be given the respect due a human, rational being. Employers, if they are really sincere, could persuade workers to accept pay-cuts in bad times, and accept fair increases in pay when times are better, as had occurred in some countries. But many employers choose to force their authority and policies down the workers' throats, being the almighty and unfeeling people they generally appear to be. As a result, much companies and organisations are suffering from industrial strife; at best, there is at least some strain in relationship or feeling of suspicion between workers and management.

The economic order of today should thus be concerned with good industrial relations and company welfarism. It is reasonable to assume here that good industrial relations and company welfarism would help to ensure productivity. It seems often the case that when a company does not do well, management blames its workers. But little do these people realise that how they manage the company plays an important part in the survival of the company; it is so convenient of them to think that they are capable managers and blame it on their workers when things are not turning out well, as has happened so often. When the general manager of a company resigns, the company could still function smoothly, but when only half the production work-force walk out, everything would be chaotic. Yet, management often regards itself as the key to high productivity and conveniently blames the worker when things do not turn out right. Should not management take the blame first before those under them are blamed? No. This hardly happens. Economists and governments should try to right this wrong approach if economics were to prove a really productive science.

Public relations and marketing would play very important roles in the economy, where business units are out to outdo each other and cut each other's throats. Even when there is no demand for a company's products or services, public relations and marketing must create awareness of these products or services in the people's minds, and ultimately the demand or greater demand for them. Marketing and public relations must be able to convince people that their products or services are better in terms of the quality, price, design, durability, etc., to create a demand or greater demand for their products or services. Many companies enrol their executives for management and marketing courses for their self-development, so that they could be more effective managers and marketers. Besides productivity and cost-saving, no company could afford to overlook the marketing aspect in today's tough business world.

But sometimes, advertising, public relations, and marketing could be carried too far and a demand for an undesirable or harmful product or service is created, which society would do better to be without. For example, the creation of too great a demand for cigarettes and liquor, both of which could bring serious health and social problems, could happen. In the author's country, because cigarettes cause cancer and other health problems, all cigarette advertisements have been banned, and cigarette manufacturers here keep a very low profile.

The classical economics of Smith, Ricardo, Mill, and the like, have been replaced by Keynesian economics, which are already being replaced by supply-side economics, which would yet be replaced in all likelihood by another brand of economics in years to come. The evolution of the science of economics goes hand in hand with the evolution of a society. Economics purports to analyse and propose solutions to the material problems of a society and intertwines with political theories and practices and social policies. Economics is concerned with the very basic needs of society, the acquisition of wealth which effects the acquisition of food, shelter, clothes and security. It is fair to say that without economic survival no other things could be made possible. No scientific advancement is possible when there is insufficient acquisition of funds for scientific research. You cannot produce good writers, scientists, astronomers, citizens, when your country is striven with vast unemployment and poverty. When there is economic chaos, you could expect crime rates to accelerate and political upheaval. That is why Keynesian theory emphasises government intervention in economic affairs, for it is ultimately the government that would be blamed and overthrown in a democratic election or, even, a coup d'etat, when it fails to solve its economic problems. Economic chaos foreshadows many other chaos in society.

It is sometimes hard to understand why there is so much unemployment in the world. There are so much problems to be solved and so much things to be done. Demand for new services or products could be created through public relations and marketing, which could mean job creation. If, hypothetically speaking, all the unemployed were employed to do social work, which is by all accounts meaningful and highly respectable work, how much social problems, not to mention the unemployment problem itself, would be solved; the unemployed could be employed, for example, in creches where they could look after the children of the employed, or they could be employed to look after the aged, the sick, the orphaned, the handicapped, the delinquent, and even the criminal, and how important and how appreciated their role would then be. It is hard to understand that while there are so much things that need to be done useful human resources are neglected by society and government. Economics should concern itself more with the social problems of the unemployed and the problems of society in general. The unemployed on their part must take up the challenge when offered such important tasks, and society must honour them for doing so.

Economic science is therefore of paramount importance. And no educated person should be allowed to be ignorant of economic reasoning. For in the last analysis, economic science helps to ensure the well-being, the survival, of the society at large. The new economics should always be concerned with new problems and, better still, it should prevent or avert new problems.

4

Greed in Practice

Wealth, which is evidently important, is essential for survival and for enjoying the finer things in life. Without money we would not have food, clothing and shelter, let alone the luxuries which only wealth could bring such as entertainment and branded goods. However, too much hankering after wealth and their trappings has apparently insensitised many to the sufferings of others and has created a bunch of self-centred beings, who are competitive, aggressive, arrogant and feel that they have to come up tops in the rat-race. In our advanced, modern society now, many people might have become so materialistic as to be ruthless, and, corrupted even.

Because of materialism, people have rushed into "get-rich-quickly" schemes and scams. Some, because of their greed for wealth, have even been conned into participation in such scams and become swindled of their money. How rich do we want to be? How much money is enough? There seems to be no limit to the yearning for wealth and riches. The more the better, it appears, as far as wealth is concerned.

Of course, the profit motive or the hankering after wealth, i.e., materialism, is the mainstay of a capitalist system such as ours. Economists may argue that this materialism is essential for economic survival and prosperity. Indeed, a person's success or status today tends to be judged by his wealth, whether inherited or acquired. It is little wonder that materialism is continually thriving. People want to earn high salaries for their work and make good profits when they are in business. Thus, job-hopping for greener pastures and profiteering could become the order of the day. Many appear hell-bent on acquiring the five Cs, viz., career, cash, country club membership, car and condominium. Many want to make lots of money and have dared to take the risks of venturing into business. The question is whether without materialism or the profit motive could the economy thrive or even survive? Materialism may be essential to a capitalist system such as ours but could have been played down.

In our pursuit of the material things in life, we may forget that we need calm, peace, security and good companionship with our fellow beings. A highly materialistic society would have many scrambling and competing with each other for wealth and riches, even to the extent of resorting to underhanded tactics such as cheating. It is disturbing to read in the papers that directors and managers of charities siphon off the funds from their charities and rogue lawyers cheat their clients or disappear with their clients' money. This is indeed materialism gone wild or overboard. Should we then tolerate or condone materialism? Our education system should step in to moderate the thinking of the people, to make the people realise that there are higher, nobler things in life than crass materialism. People should be educated to be moderate, tolerant, cooperative and sympathetic, instead of being crass, ruthless, self-centered and uncooperative. People have not only abandoned their morals, but neglected their health, even their life, in their pursuit of wealth and riches. For example, drug runners still risk their lives in smuggling drugs, a criminal offence which carries the mandatory death sentence in many countries, as they could become rich if successful in their illegal trade.

Is money, wealth or materialism all that one should look forward to in life? The poor who are contented may ultimately be happier (and spiritually richer) than the rich who are never contented. Many of the well-off and rich simply suffer from avarice when they make the worship of money or wealth their creed. Would they really prefer money or wealth over everything else, including their health or even their life? One should really have the correct perspective of things.

In conclusion, we may state that though materialism may be expected of a capitalist system such as ours, we should not allow ourselves to end up as materialism freaks, whereby we become "money-faced" and become obsessed with money and riches to the exclusion of the better, nobler things in life such as harmony, peace and contentment, easier said than done though this may be. The educational system and governmental publicity campaigns could help to inculcate in the people a balanced attitude towards the acquisition of wealth. The "soft" subjects such as philosophy and ethics evidently have an important role in this, and, there should be a new component such as business ethics incorporated into economics, the so-called science of acquiring wealth, and other business subjects. People should be concerned more about moral wealth than material wealth if they really want a happy, harmonious, peaceful society. However, the trend now seems to be gearing towards a society anxious or crazy about getting rich quick through betting, investing in stocks and shares and other "get-rich-quickly" schemes, with white-collar crime, bribery and corruption, adverse financial loss and hardship, and even bankruptcy becoming more common, which is disturbing - wealth being commonly acknowledged the root of all evils. This is evidently the result of society equating wealth with success, with successful business people being given great prominence in the media, making them the objects of envy and emulation. On the other hand, beacons of morality such as Mahatma Gandhi and Mother Theresa should be much the objects of our publicity and emulation. The problem with our capitalistic system is that we need people who are hungry enough for wealth to be willing to undertake the risks of starting businesses which provide employment and products or services for others; i.e., the profit motive plays an important part in the capitalist system, as is stated above. People go after wealth for various reasons, e.g., for survival of course, security, status, power, luxurious living, etc.. It is of course important that there is a proper balance between the acquisition of wealth and moral rectitude. Otherwise, society would in all likelihood end up having more crooks, swindlers, robbers and other social miscreants, an undesirable, fearsome consequence.

The government has an important part to play in bringing about a materially comfortable and morally upright society, in balancing the two well.

5

Technological Changes

Technology is changing so fast today that what is considered new technology would be outdated within months. What does this imply? The individual has to invest plenty of time (and, possibly, money, if he were to attend courses and seminars on the latest technologies) in learning the new technologies - he undergoes what is known as "continual education" or "life-long learning". Time away from work, which would normally be his leisure time, is devoted to this undertaking, which not only means less time for relaxation and rest, but less time for his family and friends. Is this keeping up with the technologies to be regarded as a mental challenge? I beg to disagree on this point. The mind (and body) needs rest and release from tension. Such "enforced learning" which is to be continual could build up tension, even fear of being left behind by technology, and saps up energy. It is not going to be good for our well-being in the long run; though its mental challenge could be keenly felt in the short run, the stresses and strains of keeping up could negate this "uplifting effect" in the long run, what with pressure from family members and friends who demand their attention and time, plus the nagging fear of slipping behind and not being able to keep "up-to-date on the latest". Not being able to keep up with technology might mean becoming redundant and unemployed.

From the business or company point of view, keeping up with the technologies should mean greater efficiency and being one-up over business rivals. But this inevitably entails much investment in time and money - money to purchase new equipment that is the hallmark of the latest technologies, time and money to train staff on how to utilise the new equipment and how to make use of the latest technologies. Since there is a "learning curve" when new equipment and technologies are introduced, there would be a period, perhaps a short one, of inefficiency, when the staff has to grapple with the intricacies of the new devices. What is going to be disheartening is that after the staff has mastered the new technology in the next few months, the equipment or technology is beginning to become outdated, when newer, improved version(s)/model(s) of it are being introduced. This is especially the case for computer software, which tends to be outdated within six months or so.

So, for both individuals and business organisations, the continual changes in technology means continual investment in time and money and extra effort in keeping "up-to-date with the latest". Technological changes have of course created new demands, e.g., demand for technological books, courses and seminars and demand for sophisticated systems or equipment and an high-tech, electronically enhanced life-style. Storage, retrieval and communication of information by electronic means are all carried out at unprecedented speed and scale. Are all the initial bogging down, slowness and inefficiency in embracing a new technology worth all the speed, efficiency and largeness of scale this new technology would subsequently bring? Do not forget that this new technology would be rendered relatively inefficient by the onset of a newer, better technology in the not too distant future. Generally, new technologies result in retraining of some of the staff while the rest are retrenched. A new technology generally not only boasts of speed and efficiency, but of lower manpower requirement (and, hence, lower labour costs). But do all these savings in labour, speed and efficiency outweigh the costs of investing in the new technology - investments in new equipment and training - investments which have to be continual in order to be able to keep up with the continual changes in technology? There is always a sense of uncertainty, tension, not knowing for certain where changing technology would lead everyone. Job loss and unemployment often follow the new technology.

Of course, life-styles have changed. Due to electronic networking facilities, it is possible to work from the home instead of reporting to the office to work everyday. At the push of buttons, we could turn on or off our TV sets, our doors and gates and many other devices. By the mere push of some buttons, we are able to manipulate objects, e.g., satellites, that are far out in outer space. And, many more.

It has been claimed that technology makes life easier for everyone. Is it really so? Could this be so when workers have to become grinds in order to be "up-to-date", instead of spending the time relaxing and resting, or spending more time with their families and socialising or spending their off-work time in voluntary work such as helping the underprivileged and the handicapped? Technology has changed our values. To remain employable, everyone has to learn new skills; in effect, everyone has become more self-centred - to compete well in the job market (or risk losing one's job), one has little choice but to acquire new skills and knowledge. Likewise, for the entrepreneur or the businessman to survive now, he has little choice but to acquire new technologies and engage suitably skilled staff. When would the chase for the "perfect technology" ever end? Would technology ever stop changing one day? Already many have lost their jobs because they did not or could not pick up the new skills for coping with a changed workplace. Many also have become unemployable because they did not or could not learn new skills, e.g., how to use a computer. For many, there is a fear of change, an inability to adapt to change, and a fear of or dislike for learning. Especially, the more elderly, whose habits and mindset have become fixed. This group, which might be large, is bound to suffer in this new technological age. The younger ones, especially those who just graduate from the technical institutions with the latest technical knowledge, are likely to be the ones who could adapt most easily to the current state of the technology, and they would have to keep upgrading their knowledge and skills in order to be able to ride the crests of the technological wave.

Many simple manual jobs have been taken over by machines, the result of the technological change. Before this, those with little or no education could earn a living by performing manual jobs. But even these jobs are getting scarcer and these manual workers, to survive, have to upgrade their skills to those of manning the machines that have taken over their jobs, which often require them to have some rudimental knowledge of reading and writing - they thus have to know how to perform simple reading and writing chores at least - or, they would be unemployed or unemployable.

The result of technological advancement is that sectors of the workforce have either been displaced by machines or by people who have the required skill and "leisure-time" has to be devoted to "life-long learning", which might not be fun. (What happens if one could not learn fast enough?) The job market is apparently more competitive - the number of available jobs cut down by automation or improved technology, the population growing exponentially, the technology changing faster than the rate at which it is mastered. On the surface, it appears that businesses, employers, benefit from the advanced technologies. But, even they apparently have problems keeping up, especially those with limited resources. They might save money on labour and efficiency, but all these savings might be eaten up by the further investments in technological upgrading.

On the surface, new, better technologies seem to portend a brighter, better, more exciting future. Probably, the advantage of new technology is only a myth. It seems to be something that is out of control, beyond the control of human society in general. It embroils everyone in a rat-race - race or be left behind. They say that science has never solved any problems - it only shifts the points of the problems elsewhere. This is never more evident now. Today, no one could rest on one's laurels and remain contented with what one has. One has to keep running, keep improving, to survive in the competitive world. There is much restlessness, uncertainty and insecurity. Life has lost its simplicity and has become much more complex. Is this really what we want? Or, have we been unwittingly led to this situation by circumstances beyond our control?

What would happen one day when technology evolves to the stage where it is beyond the grasp and control of the average human being, except for a minority? The ones who have invented these much complex technologies and the very few who have grasped and mastered them would have considerable powers and influence over the rest. They could be "dictators" in their own right. They might even be able to play God. Indeed, with cloning, man has already played God. This is not surprising, if you consider the fact that in any technological enterprise, the techie or technical expert is always well regarded by the big bosses - some might even have more powers than their big bosses, when they have become indispensable to their organisation - when their technical expertise and skills are well above those of all their peers.

Political power would remain in the nations with the technological clout, the leaders of technology. Even private individuals with technological clout, individuals with access to technological power, could wield considerable political power and influence. For example, Bill Gates, with his software empire, has changed the way we live and the way we are going to fight our wars.

So, is technological advancement a boon or bane to society? Doubtlessly, there have been benefits, such as better health and longer life-spans. We should not just look at these pluses, we should also look at the minuses, such as greater anxieties faced by those living in today's fast-paced world. On the whole, technology is not to be blamed. Man, who uses the technology, is the culprit.

Man must learn how to use technology intelligently and wisely, to minimise its ill-effects and maximise its advantages, rather than let it develop rampantly and run out of control. The key is to use technology to co-operate rather than to compete. But, the reverse seems to be true. Unless technology could be intelligently and wisely harnessed for the benefit of the whole of mankind, rather than just the selected ones who have the means to obtain or purchase it, leaving the rest without it to lose out or suffer in some way, technology would be more a bane than a boon to everyone. It seems that we are now more controlled by technology than in control of technology. This does not augur well for us.

Though the world economy is being fueled by technology, technology should be used wisely and with great circumspect, e.g., instead of causing fearsome job loss it should result in business expansion and job creation, the possible result of higher productivity and profitability. However, it now appears that having better technologies generally results only in being able to just compete and survive, i.e., companies have to strive harder to attain the same profitability, same result. Perhaps, the government could step in with incentives and/or subsidies to encourage such technologically advancing companies to expand and/or diversify, so that the excess labour resulting from technological change such as automation could be channeled to the new business expansion. This would be in keeping with Keynesian theory, which has advocated government intervention in times of need. At the same time, the government should also implement educational and publicity programs to encourage companies to expand and create jobs instead of cutting down jobs and retrenching when implementing automation or cost-reduction. The government should educate everyone concerned, especially the companies and bosses, to take the "macro" view, to realise that retrenchment and unemployment not only affect the employees concerned, but ultimately the whole economy - employers, employees, job-seekers, government, spending/purchasing power, etc., which are all inter-linked; the important point should be made clear to the companies and bosses that rampant retrenchment should be avoided as much as possible, for though it might help the organisation to reduce costs, it is likely to adversely affect staff morale and hence productivity, and, this loss of human productivity would in all likelihood offset the gains of better technology, better equipment (with sabotage of equipment by workers a possible "worst case" situation, which would be reminiscent of the Luddites of the First Industrial Revolution); in other words, besides the hard, technological aspect, an organisation should also pay attention to the soft, human aspect. Only then would new technologies such as automation be looked upon by workers and employees with fond anticipation of job enlargement, promotion, pay increase and higher bonus, rather than fear of being redundant and retrenched, and become really productive.

It should be noted here that new technology comes with the possibility of causing structural unemployment - unemployment resulting from workers being unable to pick up the new skills to take on the newly created jobs in a new industry while losing their jobs in a declining or "sunset" industry.

However, for society, the economy, as a whole, technology should be their servant; they should not end up being its victim. And, technology should help to boost the economy, e.g., by creating more jobs and increasing the incomes, hence, spending power, of employees, which would be an economic boon, and not take away jobs, retrench, hence reducing purchasing power, which would be a bane for the economy. The obstacle to all this is the unwillingness or inability of workers to undergo skills upgrading and retraining, which is likely to result in some structural unemployment.

In all this, the government has a very important guiding role to play.

6

Small Industries

There must be division of labour. There must be specialisation. There must be international trade or exchange. There is the necessity for inter-dependence in global affairs, be it scientific, political, economic, social, and so on. Today, industrialisation has a greater and more important role to play than in days of yore whence agriculture was the mainstay of the world's economy. Since the Industrial Revolution, things were never quite the same again - the tip of the balance in economic affairs has since been weighed down with a different emphasis. Now, we are thinking in terms of a second industrial revolution, or, for some more advanced countries, a third, or even, fourth industrial revolution.

The cardinal point is that industries have to make a start somewhere in time - since the Industrial Revolution, sweat-shops and cottage industries have evolved into bigger manufactories or manufacturing organisations, many of which have grown through the ages into private empires, or, multi-national corporations, such as Du Pont and General Motors. This entails the broad vision, daring and entrepreneurial capability of a few talented people of sharp business acumen. Of course, not everyone can be a financial genius.

For those who have seen through the tough, worrisome days of financing and running a concern, no matter how insignificant in size, it must have been quite an experience. To have a sure grasp of the intricacies of the business you are in, to dump practically all your life's savings and, probably more than that, if loans are to be taken into account, into the business, to anticipate the possibilities of making it and the pitfalls, to predict, or try to predict, public reaction to what your company specializes in, certainly are no meagre task for otherwise, each and everyone of us would be our own bosses rather than earn our own meagre living by being employed by these so-called entrepreneurs. We may think ourselves expert in any one or so of the above-mentioned fields or aspects to a commercial activity. But it would be rather a difficult thing for us to be rightly so an authority on all these. Here again, there is the question of opportunity. Born into a business family, a person may be more likely to acquire these capabilities, if he has an aptitude for it - this is likely to be due to no small part from the encouragement from the family to get involved and help out and from the sheer sense of power that can be derived from running or helping to run a business. One tends to feel that if one can run a business, runs it well and acquires much wealth, one can do almost any other thing with similar ease. This may give a false sense of security. But, nevertheless, it nurtures a self-confidence which is a prerequisite for a would-be or budding entrepreneur. It is similar to the certitude a successful insurance salesman feels about his ability to sell other things, insurance sales being one of the hardest types of sales.

It would indeed be unwise to try to do too much too quickly, as far as entrepreneurship is concerned. One cannot, for instance, if one were to invest one's capital, invest it to the extent that General Electric or Philips has done so even if one has a very vast coffer. One can only take a cautious step forward. And it may be many more years before one can really run. Alternatively, one may not be able to take this sure step forward at all; maybe, one can only crawl. One would need the technical know-how, the in-depth knowledge, one would have to learn about the market, the investment potential, one would have to consider how much risk one is prepared to take, one would have to have the capability and the means of securing loans through banks and other financial institutions. There is a myriad of other items to look into.

There is a tendency today to pay too much heed to the big, well-established corporations, many of whom are feared by governments because of their awesome power over the masses in providing jobs, training and social benefits - this puts them in a position to dictate terms to governments. It seems that people have forgotten or overlooked how they were once insignificant digits of business enterprise. Today's sweat-shop or small industry may very well be your mighty multi-national corporation of the future. But the stiffer competition, which is a direct result of the population explosion, in business, is not making it any easier to expand, or even to survive.

However, many things can be done to stimulate their growth, especially by the home government. For example, tax incentives can be given to small industries, to encourage their growth. Special training schools can be set up to train people for such industries. Interest-free loans can be made to them by the government. Quotas can even be imposed on certain imports so that these small industries are not wiped out by the much bigger competitors from abroad. Certain governments, it must be pointed out, simply believe in autarchy, and they have to put in an intense effort to see that their industries, be they big or small, thrive, though their wisdom in this respect may be doubtful; and hypothetically speaking, if by a strange twist of fate, the countries, which depend a great deal on international trade, should suddenly depend less so on international exchange, and suddenly turn to autarchy, there will result a situation whereby the world as a whole would enjoy less of the totality of goods which would only be enhanced by international trade. Though autarchy, it must be pointed out here, may make a nation less dependent on other countries, it is likely to be of less value to mankind as a whole as it is selfish and tends to create the conditions which cause international conflicts, and it also tends to impede progress for the human race as a whole because international co-operation would be lacking, under such a condition. But, in autarchies, there is a likelihood that small industries will play more important roles than would otherwise be the case; with the government's intention to make the country self-dependent, certainly, any industry, no matter how insignificant it may seem to be, would be relied upon to perform a social role in providing the necessities and goods for living; the small industries would not be likely to be taken for granted and would have a more positive role to play, and they would be an integral part of the closed economy.

Small industries vis-a-vis the bigger corporations today find difficulty competing with the latter. Obviously, difference in financial status makes all the difference. The small industries face very serious problems as a result. The big corporations have little or no problem getting loans from financial institutions because of their reputation whereas the banks would be generally more cautious about loans to the smaller companies. As the saying goes, "Money makes money". Hence, the more capital you have, the more money you can make. Expansion, for the big corporations, would hardly be a problem at all. But to the smaller companies, expansion has to be carried out with more care, due to their more limited resources.

Another factor is the difference in organisational structure. In the big corporations, a well-ordered, clearly-defined organisational structure can almost always be discerned, with many departments performing well-defined functions and very diverse functions too - hence, you may find a sports and recreation department, a public relations or community relations department, a workmen's compensation department, a safety department, or, even, as in big shipyards, a fire department. It is not surprising that some of these departments may even be bigger than a small company, in terms of sheer manpower. There is, in other words, bureaucracy, which is bad if it is over-done. Contrariwise, the staff and managers of smaller companies may be all-rounders, and over-worked all-rounders too, each performing wide and diverse functions. Because of this, there is no sense of orderliness, which turns the more ambitious employees off. This is probably because the smaller companies cannot afford to have too many departments, because they cannot afford to employ so many staff-workers. Big companies often have a reputation to live up to and preserve, hence, they have to maintain a good corporate image through their public relations department whereas a small company is a small company and over-staffing may force it to close down sooner.

Because of the vast resources available, many big corporations can afford to set up their own research and development departments. It is a case of advantages leading to more advantages. In the case of the big corporations, the advantages of wealth seem limitless. Lockheed can afford to bribe governments. General Electric can dictate terms to governments. Many can afford to employ scientists at lucrative remunerations to do nothing but think, think of better designs and better products, which can out-rival their competitors -

a scientist may only produce one or two excellent ideas in two or three years and yet such corporations find it worthwhile to put him on their payroll. At the moment in the author's country, research and development do not seem to loom large at all in corporate life and seem practically non-existent in the small industries, which, of course, could hardly afford to employ people to do nothing but think, such a seemingly unproductive activity.

The big corporations, because they provide jobs for many hundreds and thousands of people, can certainly pull the strings. They have the muscles to manipulate the economy, especially if they are conglomerates with wide-ranging business interests, employing thousands. Many are, in fact, governments in their own right. They provide you not only income if you work for them, but products and services which determine your life-styles and fashions. If you are dowdy, Lee's can make you more elegant, at least it can make you so in the eyes of fashion-conscious people who may equate elegance with Levi shirts and pants.

But, what about the small corporations, the dwarfs amongst the industrial Goliaths? They are out-shone and over-shadowed by their gigantic brethen. They generally do not enjoy the esteem of the populace, so much so that people often prefer the more expensive services and products of the bigger companies simply because they are considered more trustworthy in terms of quality standard.

Much worse than all these, the small industries, especially in the author's country, seem in great danger of being extinct. Obviously, governments encounter greater pressure from big corporations and it would be much wiser to be with the big corporations than to be against them. Many governments of Third World countries learn and import technologies from the big multi-national corporations, many of which are leaders in technology in their own right. In the light of all these, what place in society do the small industries really stand? Probably, they are at the brink of industrial death, especially so in the author's country, where they are encouraged to expand, or else, they are coerced into phasing out, what with the acquiring of private properties, old shop-houses and dilapidated factory-sites for urban renewal by the government.

Perhaps, this government is not interested in the small industries. Or, they give up hope on them. Ironically, however, many of the big multi-national corporations still turn to these supposedly insignificant industrial organisations when they are faced with production "bottle-necks" - many small industries are actually the sub-contractors of the giant corporations. The role of the small industries seems very much under-rated. But if the small industries are suddenly extinct who would be relied upon to play a supportive role in industrial society? The small and mini industries have to be nurtured and encouraged to play more important roles. Surely, by doing so, the government can diffuse some of the awesome power of conglomerates. This is the only way, perhaps, of diminishing monopoly or oligopoly power. And this is a positive benefit to consumers and society who need not unduly pay through their noses for consumer and luxury items and who can expect better quality from their purchases. The multi-national corporations do not owe any government any living. They fear practically nobody. Worse still, they are held in awe by people and governments. Why allow them to be more powerful and more fearsome by letting the small industries die? After all, the latter can act as a counter-balance economic force. We need not have to reckon with the economic power of the multi-nationals. All that would be desirable is more healthy competition from the small industries. Only with such conditions, perhaps, will the necessary evils of capitalism be diminished.

In the United Kingdom, there are over six hundred banks which specialise in serving the industries. The banks tend to favour the industrial giants, which of course is natural as they have their profit motive in doing so. The public image of small industries does not appear distinctive and it is dubious that some of them have any image at all. At best, people can only envision a rather less than positive image of such corporations. Insufficient efficiency. Lack of organisation. Haziness. These are the abstractions that tend to swamp the public mind as regards the small industries. But the ironical fact is that there are some small industrial organisations that have performed remarkably, but how many really notice them? Such an image of the small industries seems irredeemable.

It is up to a specialised agency, most probably a government agency, to salvage the image of the small industries. This should be the initial measure towards positive growth. A good public image definitely is conducive to greater marketability of products and services. The root problem of small industries is of course finance. With greater resources, presumably, most of the problems would be solved. When institutions such as the World Bank and the Asian Development Bank can devote their activities towards promoting the economic welfare of the underdeveloped and the Third World countries, why can't a government bank, or a government central bank, like the DBS, help to promote the growth of small industries by providing relatively cheap and readily available funds? A multifarious agency of the sort that is a cross-breed of the National Productivity Board, the Economic Development Board and the DBS would be ideal. There must be a conscientious drive towards nurturing the small industries, which are at the moment at the cross-roads between dying and surviving. These are all of course taken in general terms. It is idiocy to destroy the future of the small industries as it would inflict self-harm to the economy. The viability of small industries should be a desired end in itself, and as the consequences of their viability are of a national nature, the government has to formulate national policies that ensure their flourish. It is not to the national interest to nip such economic flowers in the buds. Doing otherwise would benefit everyone in every conceivable way. The small industries which are mostly local-owned should be given the opportunity to form the spine of the economy. If too much foreign investment is relied on, what would happen when foreign investment is re-channeled to other countries with cheaper labour and more relative advantages? Can we afford to run such great risks at the expense of the smaller local industries? These are disturbing questions enough; though at the moment the economic climate for foreign investment here is in peak condition, it does not mean that the government can afford to be so complacent that they treat the small industries as economic non-entities. It is essential to overhaul the public image of the small industries. The Economic Development Board has sold the author's country well to the international community; hence, the sea of foreign investments. Likewise, this proposed government agency that ought to be the saviour of the small industries should execute a blitz of public relations campaigns abroad to sell the small industries to the international community. To seek new and expand existing markets, so to speak. This must be a pre-condition for future growth.

By providing cheap and readily available loans to the small industries, it would make it easy for the small industries to conduct their own intensive public relations programs, which at the moment are practically non-existent. Once their public image is glossened, economic and financial growth is inherent. And with firm backing from a high-powered government agency as such, this is not likely to be a distant possibility.

After the paramount task of image-making, there are a host of other needs for the agency to look into. The need to train personnel for the small industries is not to be overlooked. Too often only the big corporations sponsor their staff for specialist training, to upgrade their skills. It is time that the small industries be given a helping hand to either sponsor their staff for special courses or conduct courses for their staff. A training centre can be set up for this purpose and the National Productivity Board is a good model to follow. It is the finely-honed skills of their staff that ultimately ensure the survival and expandability of the small industries.

Another aspect is technology. The big corporations are strong on computerisation. This is the age of automation, of labour-saving, cost-saving and time-saving technology. And with automation productivity is expected to improve manifold. Unfortunately, many of the small industries have stopped growing, technologically, since long back in time. The bigger industries can maximise their production with minimal costs, while the smaller organisations do not enjoy such marginal efficiency of capital. How are they to compete in the world market with outdated technology which results in high production and labour costs and second or third rate products? The conglomerates could afford to throw money on research and development and automatic and more efficient machinery. They could afford to engage the best brains to do research on better production methods and better product designs. If the small industries do not try to keep up with their bigger counterparts, they are heading for extinction. On the other hand, if they try to keep up with the pace of technological advancement, where can they find the huge chunks of funds to do so? Unless the proposed government agency provides the funds and, if possible, the facilities for research, it would only be by dint of something close to a miracle that the smaller industries can cope with the competitiveness of the industrial giants.

Obviously, the proposed agency would be saddled with a vastly complex task. They have to have the capability of convincing the small industries of the necessity for modernisation. What happens if the small set-ups are not enthusiastic about all this? Many small industries are contented with remaining small. Why ask for trouble? Why take more risks? But, if the small industries choose to remain complacent, instead of trying to modernise and improve, they may not be able to remain complacent for long; for they need not have to be complacent when they are closing down. Full government backing would be necessary. The agency, together with the government, must be single-minded in seeing the survival of the small firms. At the same time, they cannot over-play the importance of the small firms, such that foreign investors feel antagonised. Small and big companies each have their separate roles to play. There have to be nuance and subtlety in the words and deeds of the proposed agency.

It would probably be better still, if the agency has the additional mentorship of a world institution such as the United Nations or the World Bank. For it seems essential that the concept of the usefulness of the small industry and its social significance find acceptance at every level and location of human society. There should be a superfluity of activities aimed at promoting this concept and what better organisation or organisations than the above-mentioned to carry out this important public relations task.

It is hardly beyond doubt that left to themselves small industries would find survival in the dog-eat-dog economic world child's play. The author is certain that small industries are socially desirable as they provide jobs, as well as goods and services, and if they are enlarged, more jobs and more goods and services could be provided. The ultimatum of modernisation and progress for the small industries would be more of the good things in life for everybody.

To tackle these challenging tasks, the proposed agency should combine the efficiency of a banker, a trainer, a public relations manager and a marketing manager. This specialised institution may yet bring a new era in economic affairs or a new economic order.

7

World Recession and Possible Remedies

We in the democratic countries (socialist countries with controlled economies seem unaffected) are often troubled by recessions, experiencing job losses, business slow-down/liquidation and other related ill effects.

Recessions come and go in cycles and are like a dreadful epidemic. The author often wonders why we must always be helpless victims to them.

The author doesn't know whether most people are even fully aware of the causes of recession. One major cause is certainly lack of demand for goods and services. Obviously, there would be a lack of demand when people (businessmen, workers, and, even governments) "tighten their belts" (become more thrifty) out of a sense of insecurity in such bad times (they are saving more for the "rainy" days)!

Keynesian theories, which, e.g., advocate that governments spend more in order to create jobs and stimulate the economy, are normally not potent enough medicine for our economic woes.

The author would therefore like to suggest the following stronger measures:-

a) At the "micro" level, the government could pass a legislation to the effect that the business enterprises and employed individuals must spent a fixed percentage (any reasonable amount) of their earned incomes on any and whatever things they wish. Certainly, this way more demand is created, and the economy is further stimulated. This could take effect on an ad hoc basis till the economy picks up.

b) Similarly, at the "macro" level, countries, perhaps with the auspices of the UN (since there is no world government), especially those in trade blocs, could arrange to voluntarily spend a fixed percentage of their GNP on each other's goods and services for a certain period of time.

Instead of just griping about the recession in resigned helplessness, surely some of these measures could be considered, though implementing them would probably require concentrated effort and great leadership skill.

Governments could play a more positive role, as in the controlled economies.

8

Changing Jobs and Skill and Talent Distribution

Job-hopping has often ascribed to the irresponsible attitude of workers. How much truth is there in this?

Isn't job-hopping somewhat inevitable since our labour market is a free one, where the forces of supply and demand have free play?

Also, labour mobility is in some ways necessary to any economy, although it must be subject to reasonable restraint.

Entrepreneurs would not be keen on investing in a country or in expanding operations there if there was not a remote possibility of their attracting experienced workers from other corporations.

The companies which lose workers may complain but those who are hunting for workers may bask in the satisfaction of meeting their labour requirements.

Another point to bear in mind is that labour mobility helps to ensure a better spread of available talent in the country.

If favoured and important industries face serious labour shortages, the government may even encourage workers from other sectors to join such companies.

This may be called redeployment of labour but when workers move of their own accord, it is called job-hopping.

So, labour mobility is a relative thing that may be viewed differently as circumstances change.

On principle, employees should have freedom of choice just as employers have the right to hire and fire their employees.

While employees should adopt responsible work attitudes, employers should also play their part by adopting an enlightened approach to personnel management.

It is after all the employer who determines the conditions and pace of work. They can either motivate or de-motivate workers by correctly assessing skills and abilities and by reading intelligently the psychology of workers.

They should also be aware of poor human relations at the work-place which seems to be often overlooked.

Workers leave their jobs sometimes because they cannot get along with their colleagues or their bosses or both. Not everyone likes getting involved in office politics. Those who do not get into it, get out.

We should thus take a deep look at the causes of job-hopping before we begin to blame job-hoppers for their irresponsible attitude, as has often been the case.

But there are errant employers who contribute to job-hopping. Some employers may have bad attitudes too, and are not incapable of mismanagement.

To help resolve this problem of job-hopping the employers' federations and the unions could draw up codes of conduct or ethics for both employers and workers who should adhere closely to them.

After all, job-hopping is not always bad. Sometimes it is desirable, for the reasons given above.

9

Some Possible Solutions to Economic Problems

It is here proposed some solutions to our modern seemingly intractable economic problems. Keynesian theories, the bug-bear of modern economics, seem to hold little water nowadays. Modern economies appear to be in need of more radical solutions. The proposal here is an economic cure based on planned and concerted international economic cooperation. Recession, unemployment, inflation, etc., are still the scourge of modern society here and have been so for ages. Can a more effective "economic medicine" not be found that could permanently cure our economic malaise once and for all, instead of only offering a temporary cure with the expectation that the business cycle will return to taunt us in a few years?

It may be unfashionable but this is a plea that we, especially our governments, should manage the economy, instead of allowing the economy to manage us. At the macro level, we have to rethink and re-vamp our economic policies on a global scale, with nations consulting each other. The fact is that all the nations' economies are intertwined. All this signals a need for sweeping macro-economic revisions now if the status quo were to be eliminated. We should not take things lying down.

We frequently suffer the throes of economic recession, becoming the victim of the economic recession. We hope, pray, and wait helplessly for the economy to recover. Governments often try to do something that may help the economy to recover fast, but there is no guarantee that they can help bring about a reasonably quick recovery. They may introduce more public works to create jobs, implement fiscal and monetary policies, re-train retrenched workers and carry out a myriad of other actions. But the economy may take its own time to pick up. The economy seems to live a life of its own, a life that does not seem easy to control at all. In fact, the fate of the economy is the fate of all human beings. Difficulty in controlling the economy simply translates to difficulty in controlling the human destiny.

In a depressed economy, human miseries are all too obvious. The jobless are living in fear and anxiety. Many have even turned to crimes (hence, the higher crime rates may be evident), such as robbery and looting. For those who are less well off, they now have to tighten their belts, live on a smaller budget. A number might seek the assistance of the authorities. It appears a helpless situation.

From the study of the history of past economic trends, everyone is more or less telling himself that when the economy swings downwards it can be expected to swing upwards again some time in the future (perhaps, in a few years' time), and, vice versa. That is, we assume that "history repeats itself". What, if in the future, history does not repeat itself? This is not an impossible scenario. It is indeed dicey.

This chaotic state of affairs which is not new and which brings about much uncertainty and misery seems to imply something. It seems to tell us that there is something wrong with our social system. It seems to imply at least some of the following, though they are perhaps not obvious to many as they are very complex indeed:-

1) There may be a problem in the distribution of wealth. The gap between the haves and the have-nots may have become very wide.
2) People may have been "psyched" by adverse publicity into hoarding rather than spending as usual, causing a fall in demand for goods and services all round, hence, reduction in production, retrenchment and loss of jobs.
3) Too much competition and under-cutting result in loss of profitability, hence loss of incentive to produce or increase production, and, hence, business closure, retrenchment and loss of jobs.

(Competition may not be really good, though consumers tend to deem it desirable.)
4) The free enterprise system, or, the capitalistic system, without much governmental control, may not be that efficient and good after all as it implies freedom for the economic system to be well beyond proper control which enables it to move along the correct, desirable path, ending up in the wrong, undesirable direction instead.
5) The wealthy has too much power and control over the workers and the have-nots. (In a recession, the workers and the have-nots will obviously suffer more than the wealthy, who may not hesitate to displace them from their jobs to save their own skins.)
6) The bosses exploit the workers, bringing misery to the latter one way or another. Though the labour legislations protect the workers and ensure that their minimal entitlements are fulfilled, bosses can still find subtle means to exploit their workers. (This is perhaps one of the greatest flaws of the capitalist system - exploitation, greed, or, profit-maximization at the expense of the workers.)
7) The bosses may also exercise some form of subtle control over the government, e.g., by sponsoring politicians (who run the government) or threatening to re-locate to another country, thus possibly causing job loss and a poor "employment situation" (a political headache for an elected government).
8) It may be a situation that even those who are desperate for a job and are prepared to accept a low salary may have hardly any opportunity of employment. The government cannot force companies to hire anyone they do not wish to hire. (In this respect, a socialist economy has an advantage in that its government-controlled industries can provide plenty of job opportunities for the populace.)
9) Instead of being the master of technology, we may have become its slave or victim. Technology can be changing so rapidly that it is very difficult or impossible to keep up with it.
10) The economy of one nation may have been adversely affected by the economies of the others and vice versa.

It appears that capitalism is far from perfect as an economic or social system as it encourages human greed and exploitation. It may be better to combine the desirable elements of both the capitalist and socialist systems. Otherwise, we may have to reformulate a new social/economic system, which is radically different from both the capitalist and socialist systems. How about a world association to manage and co-ordinate the economies and economic activities of all the nations in the world, this association being represented by members from all the nations in the world? This association can fix or set quotas for imports and exports amongst all the world's nations. For example, the association can declare that Country A exports Item X to Country B and Item Y to Country C and imports Item S from Country B and Item T from Country C, Country D exports Item J to Countries E, F, G and H and imports Item K from Country E, Item L from Country F, Item M from Country G and Item N from Country H, etc., with the quantities imported and exported amongst them stipulated, subject to periodic changes in the future. In this way all countries in the world will have to produce sufficient goods and services to fulfill their own consumption needs as well as meet the quotas set by the association. Thus, there should be enough jobs and incomes for everyone, and, it would be a boost to the world economy and to world trade.

The author is not advocating replacing the price mechanism by the kind of state-imposed quotas and controls that produced the dire outcomes in much of the ex-communist bloc. What the author has in mind is that all the governments throughout the world consult each other and work together with each other and meet each other's requirements by achieving the import and export targets set by the proposed world economic association.

Contrary to general opinion, competition is really not good for business, especially in the long run. As mentioned in (3) above, too much competition and under-cutting may lead to business closure, retrenchment and loss of jobs, which is indeed not good for everybody. Fair enough, competition ensures that the consumer does not have to pay a high price for his good or service. Also, it is felt that competition will encourage businesses to be more productive (for example, to be more competitive or better businesses will strive to be more efficient and more cost-conscious, but they may be so cost-conscious that the welfare and safety of their workers are compromised). Cooperation and team-work amongst competitive businesses are better for there are economies of scale (resulting in cost-savings and thus, theoretically at least, lower prices for the consumer) and more heads to do the thinking and thrash ideas. However, to protect the consumer from over-priced goods or services, the government should have the right to step in and regulate prices.

Finally, a social or economic system should consider the general welfare and economic well-being or safety of every human being in the world. What we are having now is social and economic imbalance, with some people and nations having great wealth, some not so great wealth, and some having abject poverty (with problems such as famine, undernourishment and disease). Economic problems tend to lead to social problems such as crimes, riots, looting or even rebellion. The economic system should take into consideration the welfare of every human being and should not have allowed some to wallow in vast wealth while some others are down in the economic dumps. Our social or economic system should ensure a more even distribution of wealth. A more even distribution of wealth will lead to greater social equanimity.

10

More Possible Solutions to Economic Problems

This chapter raises some important points about the economy and economic policies, and proposes some important solutions. Economic problems that plague us seem intractable and seem to require some radical counter-measures. One of the root causes of a recession is that people are not spending sufficiently. To overcome this problem a radical change in our monetary system could be effected, which would complement the other conventional economic management techniques being in use.

Introduction

Economic upturns and downturns appear to happen in cycles of say three to five years, and everyone looks forward to the impending economic downturns in trepidation and helplessness. The government also apparently couldn't normally avert the economic downturn and the best it could normally do is to warn the people that the economic downturn is expected and they should be prepared for retrenchments and have to tighten their belts, and so on, becoming a sort of doomsday prophet. This is the situation of the economy controlling the people, who have become helpless victims of the economic downturn.

The crux of the matter is that money held by people has to be spent or change hands in sufficiently large volumes for the economy to be buoyant. If people lose their jobs, have little or no money to spend and curtail or stop spending the economy would be in trouble. Equally bad is the situation where employment rate is high and people have money to spend but are hardly spending. The point is that governmental policies and aggressive advertising and marketing could only try to persuade people to spend more but the final choice of whether to spend or not still belongs to individuals. This means that our economic ills would continue to be intractable unless a more radical change in the monetary system is effected to ensure sufficient spending, besides the maintenance of full employment and/or the creation of more employment opportunities and other economic measures.

Economy and Economic Policies

Economics can be defined as the science of creating wealth. It is the theoretical underpinning which explains the workings of commerce. The important point to note is that despite the analyses and recommendations of the economic experts who advise, guide and formulate governmental economic policies, the dynamics of the global economy has been as intractable as ever. Governmental policies have always been bandied about to ensure that businesses thrive, people have jobs and the economy is buoyant, but often the reverse results. What can be really seriously affecting the economy? One may wonder.

It should be borne in mind that economics is about the thinking of people involved in commerce - whether they are buying, selling, employing, looking for jobs, trading, negotiating, investing, getting bank loans, lending, etc. Companies may reduce prices, offer free gifts, increase salaries, provide all kinds of incentives, etc., to attract customers and employees, customers may selectively purchase goods based on brand-name, product image, price, service, or a combination of all these, and workers may choose jobs and employers. To modulate all these commercial activities to ensure that there is prosperity and full employment in the economy, the government has an important, central role. The government, through the central bank, can increase or decrease bank interest rates to encourage or discourage savings and hence reduce or increase the money supply, and, also increase or decrease taxes to reduce or increase the money supply. (The government influences the economy through monetary policies, which pertain to the regulation of money supply, and, fiscal policies, e.g., increasing or lowering taxes and increasing or decreasing spending on public works.)

However, what many seem not to be well aware of is that varying the interest rates and taxation rates by the government quite often does not have the desired effects - increasing or decreasing the money supply, and, increasing or decreasing spending. To expect such governmental economic policies to work all the time is naïve. Such economic policies may work sometimes, but certainly not all the time. To understand why this is so, we need to have a deeper understanding of human psychology.

Economics is actually ultimately about how people think and behave where money or wealth is concerned. There are many wealthy people who spend relatively little, and even hoard, despite their wealth, while in economic theory we assume that people with more money will spend more. On the other hand, contrary to economic theory, many not so well-off people spend relatively much despite their lack of wealth, and many may even beg, borrow or steal in order to afford a spendthrift, luxurious life-style, e.g., the shopaholics, the night-clubbers, etc. Though we may expect those with good incomes to save more when bank interest rates are high, this may not happen when the person is spendthrift and generous, e.g., interested in shopping, traveling, dining in fine style, clubbing and giving treats. Some of these people may have other financial commitments, e.g., mortgages to pay, children's education to finance, loans to repay, investments or other business undertakings, etc.; so they may not be able to save despite the high bank interest rates. Of course, those with lower incomes, who are less able to make ends meet, may also not be inclined or able to save even if the bank interest rates were very high.

High import duties and taxes may also not coerce people to spend less. For instance, despite the high import duties, road taxes and electronic road pricing (ERP) charges for cars to discourage car-ownership, making car-ownership in the author's country really expensive, many who can ill afford to own cars possess them, for the love of the automobile, convenience and/or the sake of looking good (status symbol). Despite all the best efforts of the government here to reduce the car population in order to solve the problem of road congestion, car-ownership seems to be getting more robust. And, despite the high import duties and hence high prices of liquor and cigarettes here, those addicted to them evidently continue consuming them as before. We should also not under-estimate the effect of advertising or marketing gimmicks, which can be subtle but can cause impulse buying, especially in the case of consumer products such as food, drinks and clothing - here people who purchase are governed more by emotion or feeling than reason and may do so whimsically.

Also, do not be surprised that often the not so well-off will spend more than the rich. It must be noted that immaterial of whether they are wealthy or poor some people will simply spend, as it is their nature to be spendthrift and generous with money. Some people may just lack financial management skills and discipline where budgeting is concerned while some others are prudent and wise with their money. On the other hand, many wealthy people are miserly or "Jews" as they may be derisively called. That is, the wealthy, who are expected to spend more, or, save more, or, invest, may not do so, while many who are not well-off may spend a great deal, some even borrowing or stealing to do so.

There are also well-to-do people who think far ahead, plan and save for a great future or for the "rainy day" instead of spending freely. There are also people with entrepreneurial ambitions who may save in order to start a business, regardless of the bank interest rates and taxation rates. There are people who live simple lives, who will save a substantial part of their income because they have no interest in shopping, fine-dining, clubbing, traveling and other luxuries.

Evident Solution

Doesn't all this explain the frequent failures of governmental monetary and taxation policies where the economy is concerned? Too little money circulating, i.e., too little spending, in the economy leads to depression and unemployment. Too much money circulating, i.e., too much spending, leads to inflation or high prices and financial hardship. However, there is an evident solution to all this. To solve the problem of depression, people can be "forced" to spend in order to increase the money supply and buoy up the economy. Here, two types of currency can be introduced, one type with expiry dates (similar in principle to gift vouchers, which sellers who receive them from buyers will exchange (redeem) for currencies without expiry dates (or with a certain percentage of them in currencies with expiry dates) from the governmental authority managing the whole system), which may be varied, to ensure that a certain quantity of money circulates during a certain period (these money have to be spent by certain dates and cannot be saved), the other type with no expiry date which can be spent anytime or saved. (Introducing the currency with expiry dates may be too daunting to be carried out at the initial stage. Perhaps, for a start, introducing the use of gift vouchers (with expiry dates) can be done, which may not be so daunting, and progress from there gradually to the adoption of the currency with expiry dates. In fact, gift vouchers with expiry dates and currency with expiry dates are somewhat equivalent. However, some countries may prefer to stick with gift vouchers with expiry dates, but the gift vouchers may not be taken seriously as they are not currency with legal standing.) The expiry dates of the first type of currency can be varied as follows: short, medium or long term in expiry. The expiry dates can be adjusted from time to time according to the economic conditions. For example, if there is inflation, i.e., too much money is in circulation, the currencies with expiry dates may, for instance, specify that the money cannot be spent for the next few months/years (period), after which period they can be spent but will expire on certain dates. By thus playing around with the usage and expiry dates of these currencies, the amount of money, and spending, in the economy can be controlled. On the other hand, to counter the effects of deflation, wherein the quantity of money in circulation and spending is low, the expiry dates of these currencies can be shortened. However, in this instance, to avert the onset of inflation the production of goods and services should keep up with the increased demand caused by the increase in money supply and spending.

All this should be administered by a statutory body or governmental body. Employees and workers, and, sellers (sellers must accept the currencies with expiry dates from their customers since they are legal tender and will redeem the currencies with expiry dates from the government for currencies without expiry dates (or with a certain percentage of them in currencies with expiry dates) as is described above - sellers will also as usual continue to accept currencies without expiry dates), will thus be paid with two types of currencies, one with the above-mentioned expiry dates and the other without. What amount or proportion of the two types of currency to be paid out should be determined and administered by this statutory body or governmental body, based on the economic conditions and/or forecasts for the specific period. Neater still if instead of paying by issuing these two types of hard currency a debit card (payment based on the actual amounts of the two types of currency available in the person's debit card account, which will be deducted from the account when the account holder is making payments) is used; this debit card or cashless paying method should make it easier for the governmental institution to administer the whole monetary system. This will apparently be an effective way to overcome our on-going economic malaise over which we seem to have little or no control - depression, unemployment, inflation, deflation. Here we are only talking about monetary transactions within the same country. However, the actual details for the implementation of the whole scheme should be carefully worked out.

For example, in the author's country, people with lower or no incomes have been given spending vouchers with dominations of two dollars and expiry dates, normally a booklet of 25 vouchers of domination of two dollars each giving a total of 50 dollars (equivalent to money), by the government which they could use to make purchases at designated stalls or stores that are participants in this scheme implemented by the government, wherein the stall or store owners who receive the vouchers from their customers would redeem the vouchers for solid cash from the government; this is apparently a scheme to financially help the people with lower or no incomes as well as to boost the economy at the same time. The author also knows of a large corporation in his country, which is government-linked, which had paid its employees bonuses in the form of gift vouchers (with expiry dates), with its chief executive officer saying this would help boost the economy.

At the international level, concerning trading between countries, the same principle should also apply, except that the currencies with expiry dates, the currencies without expiry dates and the debit cards should now be issued and administered by an international authority, e.g., a newly created division of the United

Nations. Here, it may be more complicated but the details can be worked out by the parties concerned.

Summing up on the point why economics does not solve economic problems, it can be said that economics fail because people's minds, attitudes and behaviours are evidently very difficult, if not impossible, to predict. As is described above, they are complex and come in a great variety of types and characters, often emotional and not very rational, and full of whims and fancies which are quickly changing as well as habits, and therefore cannot be expected to respond appropriately to governmental economic policies which are based on assumptions that may be too simplistic and unrealistic. However, the monetary system described above should perform the trick. This new monetary system should help to eradicate recessions, unemployment and other economic and related social problems.

In any case, we should control the economy and not let the economy control us, and, by the above-described technique the economy may be controlled.

11

Economic Problems, Capitalism and Possible Solutions

Much has been said about capitalism and capitalists. Capitalists are often viewed as grubby, shrewd and unscrupulous especially where money is concerned. The capitalist economic system depends on their investments to thrive. This chapter looks at economic principles, economic problems and the part capitalists play to keep things going in the capitalist economic system, offering some possible solutions to economic problems.

Introduction

The world has long been beset with economic problems such as inflation, deflation, stagflation, unemployment, poverty, recessions and conflicts between workers and bosses, all of which have apparently still not been solved. Could these problems ever be solved? This chapter analyses the problems and offers some suggestions for their possible solution.

Analysis and Possible Solutions

Economics is apparently common sense. As someone the author knows who is an economics graduate remarked, economics is common sense made difficult. (It is apparent that this economic common sense has to be made difficult, through systemisation, etc., so that it would be a subject worthy of academic study, for if it is pure, inherent common sense, which every normal human being should possess, there is no need to study economics.)

In the capitalist system, the government apparently does not intervene much (unlike the case of socialism, where enterprises are state-owned or state-controlled) unless it is necessary, letting the market forces of demand and supply play their part. In Keynesian theory, the state is supposed to create jobs and boost the economy by carrying out public works, i.e., intervene in the economy, but only when necessary.

The capitalist system has more to do with free enterprise, letting the market forces of demand and supply work freely to affect and influence prices of goods and services, without the unnecessary intervention of the government, which may of course lead to problems such as inflation, deflation, stagflation, etc.; it plays on the profit motive, or, to put it more bluntly greed, of the entrepreneur.

On the other hand, the socialist system involves central or governmental control of businesses, wherein businesses are state-controlled and state-owned. But socialist countries such as Russia and China have been deviating towards a more capitalist system, which has apparently helped their respective economies to open up and expand quickly, resulting in many millionaires and billionaires, and also the social ills associated with great wealth in the hands of the relatively few.

It would be good to have the combination of the desirable elements of both the capitalist and socialist systems. The capitalist system may be good in that it encourages initiative and creative thinking, and, this combined with the control/direction of the state government which ensures that businesses are ethical and good corporate citizens, and that businesses are conducted in such a way that it would be a win-win for the business, the consumer, and the country as a whole.

Importantly, state or governmental control should, as the master-mind, see that the economy as a whole functions smoothly, with minimal unemployment, more equitable distribution of wealth and minimal poverty, depression free, etc.

There are much vaunted economic problems, some of which are serious unemployment, under-employment even, highly unbalanced distribution of wealth, world poverty and its related social problems, and so on. Such economic problems have often been hard to manage and overcome (their management and solution being the responsibility of the state), resulting in hardship to the common man who could end up jobless and without income and the government being blamed for failing to bring prosperity and economic well-being to the country which may result in it being booted out in the next election.

Economic upturns and downturns appear to happen in cycles of say three to five years, and everyone looks forward to the impending economic downturns in trepidation and helplessness. The government also apparently couldn't normally avert the economic downturn and the best it could normally do is to warn the people that the economic downturn is expected and they should be prepared for retrenchments and have to tighten their belts, and so on, becoming a sort of doomsday prophet. This is the situation of the economy controlling the people, who have become helpless victims of the economic downturn.

Such economic downturns should not be allowed to happen, resulting in retrenchments, unemployment, businesses closing down, in short misery. The economy should be controlled, or better controlled, in other words, *better managed*, to prevent all these undesirable economical things which cause hardship.

We should control the economy and not let the economy control us, i.e., the government, should manage/control the economy well and *prevent* recessions, retrenchments, unemployment, inflation and other economic hardships from happening, for such hardships would have adverse effects on society.

One way of achieving this desirable economic outcome is possibly by having a world association of nations which carries out economic cooperation with this aim in mind. However, the developed countries might not be keen to participate in the proposed world association of nations for economic cooperation, which is not surprising. If they think there is little or no benefit in participating, they would of course not participate, which is human nature. Even some underdeveloped or developing countries might not be keen to participate. Some countries might even think the proposed world association would not work (that is, they have no confidence that this proposed world association would work out) and thus would not join the world association.

There are already regional groups for economic and other forms of cooperation, e.g., the European Union, ASEAN, NATO, etc. Of course, for this proposed world association for economic cooperation, starting with countries in the region, which have perhaps more similarities in their cultures, would be easier. Maybe, some less developed countries from the Middle East could form this world association for economic cooperation and make it a success. If it is successful other countries would probably be interested in joining the world association.

The developed nations might not be interested in such a world association for economic cooperation as they probably would not be keen to share their economic success with the less developed nations. However, they should realise that many of the undeveloped and underdeveloped nations have natural resources which the developed countries might not have. For example, an underdeveloped nation such as South Africa is rich in minerals and agriculture, e.g., cocoa, gold, diamonds, etc., while some developed nations have little or none of such natural resources. Thus a developed nation with little or no natural resources refusing to do business or cooperate economically with an underdeveloped nation rich in natural resources such as South Africa might lose out.

Such a world association for economic cooperation might not be able to get the full agreement and cooperation of all the nations for various reasons, which could be expected. Even if a few nations agree to cooperate for a start, it would be good. If this turns out a success, more nations could be expected to join in. Theoretically, this world association is a means to controlling and managing the economy (which is a noble objective), and not vice versa as is the current situation apparently.

There have been other forms of international economic cooperation, e.g., the European Union, ASEAN, GATT (General Agreement on Tariffs and Trade), GSP (General System of Preferences), etc., besides the world associations such as the UN and WTO. So, how is this proposed world association not possible? Economies might turn out so badly, e.g., having world depression, stagflation, and so on, that nations could be coerced into working together for the common good. If they don't try to work together they might not be able to overcome serious economic problems or achieve economic success. However, some of these trade blocs are protectionist, i.e., they give preferential treatment to their own bloc members, while others doing business with them would lose out without this preferential treatment, such as finding their products comparatively more expensive and thus less competitive.

It is emphasised here that there should be better control or better management of the economy by the government to prevent economic hardships such as recessions, unemployment, retrenchments, inflation, businesses closing down, poverty, etc. These economic hardships, depressions, recessions, unemployment, poverty, and so on, appear to be taken for granted, as though nothing much could be done to avert them. Something should and could be done to avert these economic hardships; people should not be helpless and at the mercy of the economy and its behaviour.

In the past, socialism and communism had been quite popular as they appeared to promise more equality, and, the democratic countries had been worried about socialism and communism taking over the democratic countries through the "domino effect". But now Russia and China, the major socialist/communist countries, have suddenly become more capitalistic, reverting somewhat to their earlier economic/social system of landlordism and capitalism. It appears that capitalism, to these socialist/communist countries, is the fastest way to get rid of poverty and to increase the standard of living of the people. Socialism or communism, wherein businesses are state-owned and state-controlled, would apparently have brought about more social equality, more equal distribution of wealth in society; it would strongly appeal to those who treasure equality as it did at one time in the past.

These socialist countries turning more to capitalism appears to imply that the lure of wealth or greed for wealth is still the best motivator for entrepreneurs to take business risks, and thereby fast economic progress is achieved as a result. Of course some of these countries would achieve more economic success than others due to factors such as good government, good management, hardworking, enterprising citizens, human talent, natural resources, and even luck.

Some might think that the only way to change a failing, problem-ridden economic system is through the revolutionary way. However, governments would never allow revolutions (whether armed or unarmed), which would not only imply they are no good, it would also be illegal under the state laws. In a democracy, if the government is not good, with problems such as corruption, nepotism and poor economic and other forms of management, the normal, legal way is to vote it out in the elections. It would be a revolution, or coup d'tat, if some military strongman takes over the government by force, as has often happened in some countries. In the case of communist China, in the 50's or so, the peasants under the leadership of Mao Tse-tung had revolted against the government and took over.

Perhaps only when the government really oppresses the people and does not really take care of them, when the people have no jobs, not enough food, no proper shelter, and are suffering greatly, would the people be motivated to show their unhappiness to the government by holding demonstrations or rioting. They would not be able to take over the government by force, as the government is normally backed by the military, unless they are able to take up arms whereby they would become armed rebels or revolutionaries. Apparently, only serious oppression of the people by the government and the intensive suffering of the people could lead to the people revolting.

Thus, achieving economic success by revolution, even a peaceful revolution, is apparently not easy. Influencial economists such as Keynes, Schumpeter, Hayek, etc., use theory, reasoning, persuasion, publicity to influence economic policies and help solve economic problems. Some like Keynes also happened to be official government economic czars, holding influential official positions in government. Keynes had also written some influencial economics books; Schumpeter and Hayek, etc., had also written influencial economics books. Revolution implies using force to get the authorities to change to what is considered the correct or proper way, when people normally don't like to be forced but wouldn't mind being persuaded. Persuasion is also not easy, e.g., persuading someone to accept a theory which one is confident would bring the required results. Marx spoke about dialectics, debating about ideas which clash and coming up with better ideas. Maybe reasoning, debating, persuasion, influencing (perhaps through holding some position of influence such as in the case of Keynes) and writing books (Marx wrote his magnum opus "Das Kapital" on which socialism and communism are based) or pamphlets could help to bring about the desired, proper changes to the world economy. Perhaps, becoming a government or political leader is the fastest and most direct way to change the economy for good, and, this might even be easier than carrying out a revolution, as it is legal while a revolution may not be legal and may have to be carried out stealthily or secretly.

The revolution described might be only a revolution in ideas, when new ideas replace existing ideas. However, implementing the new ideas might require difficult systemic changes, which the government might not be willing to shoulder (people generally do not like changes and would prefer to stick to their customary ways of doing things).

Marx could be said to be a revolutionary in thought. Whereas in the feudal society, the power had always been with the ruling class and elites, who were powerful and wealthy, e.g., capitalists or business people (bourgeois), characterised by authoritarianism, abuse and corruption, his revolutionary ideas suggest that the power should rest with the working class (proletariat). Based on Marx's ideas that the working class should rise up and dominate, came socialism and communism, wherein every aspect of the economy is state-controlled and state-owned, for the people and by the people. But this appears to have given rise to a new class of elites, namely the officials running the state organs. Marx's ideas appear to have happened at the right time when there had been rampant poverty, suffering and abuse by the elites; hence their success.

In the present society, there is always the looming problem of unemployment, under-employment, and the related economic hardships such as poverty, famine, etc. Thinking aloud, people, who have energy, skills and talents, shouldn't be allowed to stay unemployed or under-employed, for there are so many problems in society whereby their labour, skills, talents, and even dedication to society, could be utilised to solve these problems. People might not be able to find jobs in business enterprises and organisations whereby they have no income and face financial hardships. Ask these people why they need to work, practically all of them would say they need to work to earn an income in order to survive. How many would say they need to work because they want to serve and help society, i.e., they want to be useful?

There are so much societal problems, which need to be tackled, e.g., now the Covid-19 pandemic ravaging the people, climate change problems, spontaneous fires burning down the environment and properties, floods, drug abuse, delinquency, criminal acts, the elderly in need of home care, the young ones in need of home care while their parents go to work, traffic congestions, calamities, and many more. Couldn't these unemployed or under-employed, many of whom might even be highly qualified and skilled, be engaged by the government as "society welfare officers" to provide public services such as disease control for Covid-19 as social distancing officials, swabbers, etc., fighting fires in the case of spontaneous fires, providing in-home/out-home care for the elderly and the young whose parents have to go to work, help to clear/develop land for agriculture, building or other infra-structure constructions, help to build dams and clear drainage canals to prevent floods, provide free tuition and other help to underprivileged youths/students in need of academic and other aids, help to direct and control traffic to prevent traffic congestion, act as vigilantes looking out for delinquents, drug abusers, potential criminals and criminals (crime-prevention), potential terrorists and terrorists, etc., attend to any contingency problems in society, e.g., those caused by hurricanes and earthquakes, etc., even advise the government on certain aspects of society if they really have the expertise/qualifications, and many more. These would be meaningful work practically all people would feel happy and proud to carry out (instead of working in a company, helping the owners to create wealth and become rich, possibly at one's own expense, e.g., being paid unfair wages for unfair amount of work (i.e., suffer exploitation), and at the beck and call and mercy of the owners, being enslaved by them). Exploitation of workers has always been a problem of capitalism, and there is always conflict between the workers (represented by unions) and the employers, a problem which Marxism acknowledged and attempted to tackle.

According to probably the most influential economist of the 20th. century, Keynes, the government could solve the serious problem of unemployment by creating jobs through carrying out public works. If the author recalls correctly, he even said the government could employ the jobless to dig trenches in order to earn an income, perhaps jokingly.

Because we are living in a capitalist society, problems of capitalism are encountered and we suggest solutions for them within our capitalist system. If we live in a socialist society and encounter the problems of socialism we also suggest solutions for them within our socialist system. The interesting question is whether we can use socialist methods to solve problems of our capitalist society, or, if living in a socialist society use capitalist methods to solve problems of socialism? It probably could be done. However, some might insist we can't rely on a failed or failing economic system like our capitalistic system to solve our economic problems. What economic system could be relied on for settling our economic problems?

On the question of human labour being replaced by automation, robots and AI, this is apparently due to the desire of companies to maximise profits by increasing productivity and reducing costs, particularly labour costs, which is the hallmark of the capitalist system. Workers, through their unions, keep pressing for higher wages, allowances and other fringe benefits, taking all kinds of leave such as vacation, medical and compassionate leave, requiring rest time, reluctant or refusing to perform certain types of work, e.g., shift work, work deemed dangerous, etc., and express their unhappiness with company policies, creating headaches for the human resource department and the company. Labour might also be difficult to recruit. As a result, the profitability of the company suffers. The company thus turns to automation and robots to solve all these employee problems, cut costs, increase productivity and thereby increase profitability. Automatons and robots do not take leave, do not demand for better wages, allowances and benefits, do not complain, and work much faster and with much greater precision, though they may break down if not properly maintained. Who is to be blamed, the employees or the employer? Because of automation, robotisation and AI, many jobs are lost forever possibly resulting in structural unemployment.

If people lose their jobs to automatons, robots and AI and could not find jobs due to the lack of technical skills for the high-tech jobs in the modern economy, they would not be able to live decently without an income. This trend of people losing jobs and displaced in this way and being unable to find new jobs might become common. There have been suggestions for the government to provide a universal basic income for people displaced from their jobs and unable to find new jobs due to the lack of the required skills or other reasons.

It is apparent that capitalism has its many problems, e.g., recessions, depressions, unemployment, retrenchments, inflation, deflation, stagflation, exploitation, great disparity in the distribution of wealth, poverty, and so on.

On the other hand, socialism or communism, which has aimed at more equality for the working class, has turned to capitalism apparently to improve the people's standard of living and reduce poverty, probably implying that the desire for wealth or profit is the greatest motivator for business expansion and thereby economic growth. If capitalism were really so bad, why did the socialists and communists, e.g., Russia and China, who had at one time violently denounced capitalists, e.g., powerful landlords many of whom had been stoned to death by the people when communist China first came into power, make an about-turn and embrace capitalism now, producing many millionaires and billionaires among their citizens, a number of which are in the Forbes' list of wealthiest persons in the world?

Would an economic system combining only the desirable elements of both the capitalist and socialist systems be the answer to settling our economic problems? Some radicals might even favour autarchy, a system wherein a country is completely independent; the country produces and makes everything themselves and does not depend on or trade with other countries. Could some economist or theoretician come up with a better economic system than the capitalist and socialist systems? The system wherein a universal basic income is given to every citizen, so that no one would end up a beggar, has already been under consideration. There is a possible problem with universal basic income. If everyone has an income and could have a decent living without working, relatively few people would want to look for jobs. If people are idle and refuse to work or work hard in the economy, imagine what is going to happen to the economy. Then how is the revenue to be generated for paying the universal basic incomes if people don't work and companies can't produce much and the government can't collect much taxes?

The problem is that economics is not an exact science, though there have been many ideas from economists and theoreticians. For example, there had been a proposal about giving every citizen some capital to invest, which is interesting. But not everyone could be or is interested in being an entrepreneur.

Some are risk averse. Some even look down on entrepreneurs regarding them as not very bright people and not capable of great intellectual work like the scientists; in fact, one doesn't need much education or training to be an entrepreneur - entrepreneurs are normally risk takers who are hard up for wealth and big bucks. Possibly many would like to have this capital for investment as they like the idea of being their own boss so that they won't have to see their hateful boss's face anymore.

Capitalism is sometimes portrayed as a modern form of slavery and feudalism. There appears to be some truth in this. Capitalists, particularly the big ones, could be very powerful and could dictate terms to the government. Society has apparently progressed from a feudal one to a democratic one, but democracy could subtly be feudalism in disguise. There was a book published one or two years ago whose author claims that companies are actually, and subtly, the government of the people. As most people spend most of their awake time working in companies, they are governed by the rules and regulations of their companies, apparently more so than by the rules and regulations of their actual democratically elected government. In fact, practically all of us are at the mercy of our employers who have every right to hire and fire us, i.e., they could deprive us of our livelihoods according to their whim and fancy, just like the past feudal lords lording over their subjects. Capitalists could thus be regarded as neo feudal lords, who are also frequently slave drivers pressing their workers to work harder and harder for more and more profits. The above-mentioned idea of the government giving citizens some capital to invest on their own might overcome this "enslavement" problem. People could use the money to set up some small business and be their own boss and so "don't have to see the boss's face". Some of them might even use the money to invest in stocks and shares to make some quick bucks, but are likely to end up losing all their capital.

Because of the many ills of capitalism, socialism and communism were popular at one time in the past. Theoretically at least, in a socialist society the working class was supposed to hold power and not the capitalists. Apparently, under socialist or communist rule, in the past people had lived simple lives with little or no luxuries, e.g., without cars, CD players, etc., the common mode of transport being bicycles. Now they have all these luxuries and could even travel round the world. They have become liberalised, i.e., they have more freedom. Perhaps it is basic human nature to want more luxuries and freedom. Hence the apparent reversion to capitalism where more money could be earned for enjoying the various luxuries such as cars, travel, etc. If people had stayed contented with the simple life with little or no luxuries, would there be a need for capitalism in a socialist or communist society?

However, even in capitalist societies not too many could afford luxuries, or even necessities, because of poverty, which is a big issue. The term "capitalism" implies using capital or money to produce goods and services and create prosperity and wealth. But unfortunately in capitalist societies not everyone is wealthy, with there apparently being great disparity of wealth amongst the people.

We have to carry out commercial activities and trade to survive, either as an employee or entrepreneur, e.g., when people are sick they need the service of a doctor, when they need shelter they need a building contractor to build houses for them, who would engage construction workers, when we need food and clothing, the manufacturers would make them for us by engaging production workers, etc. So both workers and entrepreneurs (who take the risks of setting up the businesses while most others are either risk averse or have no capital, or both) are necessary in the economy. The problem with the economic systems is that there is always conflict between the workers and the entrepreneurs, when both are necessary for the economy to produce goods and services, i.e., there is as usual, as Marx called it, a class struggle. If this "class struggle" could be straightened out, it would be better for society.

For workers not to be underdogs in the economy, they should be given some say in the running of companies. Probably, this is only possible in socialist societies where companies and businesses are state-owned and state-controlled, for the people and by the people, wherein the workers may elect their representatives to be members of the company's board of directors, who may elect the managers from among themselves to run the company or employ someone else from outside the company who have the necessary experience and qualifications to operate the company (perhaps similar in democratic principle to the British parliamentary system wherein the people elect the MPs to parliament and the MPs among themselves elect their prime minister who appoints his cabinet ministers from among the MPs in the parliament).

Capitalists enjoy privileges and would not easily give up their privileges, which implies people basically enjoy wealth and power, would like to exercise their power over others, ordering their underlings around and so on. Workers may complain about bullying and exploitation by their capitalist bosses. But when they become bosses themselves they may also become bullies, maybe even bigger bullies and exploiters. This may be an eternal, unsolvable human problem.

Many foreign countries have their products manufactured in China because of its cheap and plentiful labour and a very large market with a population of 1.6 billion or so. But many businesses set up in China to take advantage of its cheap and easily available labour had initially made losses there as the Chinese copied their products and manufactured them themselves. However, this problem appears to have been overcome when the Chinese were given a share in the business by the foreigners setting up there.

Though capitalists might be exploitative and unethical, they are a necessary evil in society. If they don't set up companies to produce goods and services, there would be no jobs and no products and services, i.e., people have no incomes, society can't enjoy their products and services and the government has no revenue as there are no workers' incomes and company profits for the government to tax. If they move their investments out of the country, there could be a massive unemployment problem for the government to handle. The big multi-national corporations which provide many thousands of jobs could thus hold the government at ransom by threatening to move their investments out of the country. Capitalism, by the way, works on the basis of greed, greed for wealth; when people become greedy, which is normally not considered a good quality, they would attempt to acquire as much wealth as possible by all means, both legally and probably illegally, including bribery, and ethically and unethically, even possibly harming or murdering their business rivals, not to mention exploiting and slave-driving their workers, even cheating on taxes by under-declaring profits, selling drugs which cause harm to society, etc. They become money-faced - no money no talk. This characteristic of greed also appears to be a common human characteristic found everywhere and in all societies, e.g., in socialist countries such as communist China where top communist officials have been imprisoned or executed for corruption and accepting bribes. So it might not be the economic system or the economic idea that fails but the fault or weakness of the human character causing the economic system to fail. Perhaps capitalism should be acceptable and palatable if it is practiced by business people with good character, e.g., with kindness, empathy, honesty, humaneness, etc., good ethics and good professionalism, such as honest hard work for honest money, which seems a rarity.

If capitalism is undesirable, there are other alternatives, e.g., socialism, autarchy, autocracy, and other new economic ideas. New economic ideas might look good on paper but might be difficult to implement, and people, whose cooperation is important, might be reluctant to welcome them (change has always been hard to accept as people normally prefer to stick with the customary way of doing things). New economic ideas, during implementation, might have to be quickly modified to suit the current situation, and quickly discarded and replaced by new ideas when found really not able to bring results. Marxism had looked good and its ideas, under socialism, have been implemented but now appears to have been revised by the socialist countries to include capitalism. There have been countries which are only partially socialist, e.g., democratic socialist countries. Theoretically, socialism probably looks best and fairest, whereby the ills and problems of capitalism would be absent. But the socialist system could be mismanaged by those running the system, e.g., through corruption, nepotism, etc. So, if the socialist system is properly managed it should work - it is thus possibly not the weakness of Marx's socialist ideas but the weakness of character of the officials manning the socialist system causing the failure of the system, viz., human failure.

Many, perhaps practically all, elected political leaders are from the elite classes, e.g., business men or capitalist class, professionals, highly educated class, and so on. Politics is apparently more for the wealthy and highly educated (wealth and high education are also apparently linked for tertiary education is costly and only the wealthy could afford the high fees of tertiary education for their children, even engaging tutors and coaches to help their children excel in exams, earn top grades, and enter and graduate from elite universities). Participating in elections requires a lot of money, e.g., for the election campaigns, the deposits for standing for election, etc., which only the well-to-do could afford. So being from the elite class, especially the capitalist class, wouldn't their sympathies be with their elite class of capitalists and the well-to-do when they hold political office? Do not expect a poor, jobless but nevertheless capable man to participate in elections, though there had probably been a few exceptions.

Capitalists might be unethical, e.g., they might exploit workers, over-charge customers, short-change customers, under-declare their taxable incomes, etc. However, they should be accorded some credit for helping to grow the economy. At least they have the guts or courage to invest their money in a risky commercial venture, while the rest of the people have cold feet and/or lack the capital to do so and would be jobless with no incomes if not gainfully employed by them. The general observation is that the more highly educated, e.g., those with degrees, etc., normally prefer to choose the safer way to make a living, such as working in a multi-national corporation as a corporate executive with a good salary, while those with lower education, e.g., high school level below, who are likely to find the corporate jobs with good salaries out of their reach, are more prepared to take risks and venture into entrepreneurship as they apparently have much to gain if the business succeeds and relatively little to lose if the business fails. It is apparent that entrepreneurship is highly risky and pressurising. Business men have been known to spend sleepless nights worrying about business failure. But the rewards are great if the business succeeds; normally, the higher the risks are the greater would be the profits earned. The poor might have zero wealth, but a failed business man seriously in debt and sued for bankruptcy could end up worse than the poor if made bankrupt for he would then end up with negative wealth. That is the reason some businesses try to avoid such liability by making their companies private limited, i.e., their liability is limited only to the assets of their companies while their personal assets are free of liability and untouchable in the event that the business fails and might be declared bankrupt. Under such high risk circumstances, not many dare to venture into entrepreneurship. Some might even think that a person has to be not that bright, even a fool, not to be aware of the high risks of business, to venture into business, while the bright, smart ones, e.g., perhaps the more highly educated, who are perhaps more capable of anticipating the risks and dangers of entrepreneurship, would avoid it. However, it is probable that those who venture into business are aware of the risks involved, but they have the courage to take risks, while others might be risk averse, and they might think that they have nothing or little to lose if the business fails, e.g., the less highly educated person might think this way as the opportunity costs of venturing into business for him would not be that high (as compared to the more highly educated person, with degrees, who could otherwise earn a high salary by working in a corporation).

Imagine this: If the government gets rid of entrepreneurs because their greed and lack of ethics cause problems in society, what is going to happen to society? Would the others in society who are employees or self-employed, who might be risk averse and/or lacking in capital, take over or be willing to take over the roles of the entrepreneurs? Entrepreneurs not only provide jobs and incomes to the people and incomes to their suppliers, they also provide goods and services, some of them essential, e.g., essential drugs for fighting diseases, etc., as well as revenues to the government who tax their company profits and their employees' and suppliers' incomes? Can society really survive without entrepreneurs? Apparently, governments are more afraid of the entrepreneur than the ordinary common man as they hold such powers in society. Unless the government is prepared to take over the apparently important roles of the entrepreneurs, e.g., the socialist governments which control all the industries and businesses in the country, or other more ethical and professional people are prepared to take over, the entrepreneurs have to stay to continue playing their important roles in society. According to the economics text-books, the factors of production are land, labour and capital. Perhaps entrepreneurship should also be considered a factor of production though this might be subject to dispute - entrepreneurship implies initiative and leadership, besides risk-taking, exercised by the entrepreneur, which are important, even essential, to the business.

However, there could be some people who are strongly and passionately against capitalism. If capitalism were to be replaced, what system would they suggest as a replacement? There may be a better economic system than capitalism, which is possibly waiting to be created by a new Karl Marx.

If capitalism is really bad and doesn't really bring benefits to the people, why would more and more countries, including the big socialist countries like Russia and China, embrace capitalism? If capitalism is so disliked, why don't the citizens complain, demonstrate, riot and ask their governments to disband capitalism, why don't the masses write to the media and forums to complain, if possible every day, about capitalism? Many workers could be heard complaining about their bosses' bullying behaviours and being exploited by their bosses. Apparently they only complain about the capitalists but not the capitalist system itself. Couldn't it be inferred from this that the capitalist system is fine and acceptable in principle, as it should be as it is a free enterprise system which rewards risk-taking, initiative and hard work and doesn't limit the freedom of the workers and the bosses to change their social status (i.e., there is social mobility, whereby many workers have worked their way up to become bosses and millionaires even themselves - maybe this could be called meritocracy; in the slavery system of the past, did the slaves have any chance to be the masters and owners of slaves at all?), and it is only the people using the capitalist system who are not using the system properly? Who would complain about capitalism when everyone has the chance to climb up the social ladder and be a boss if only he were willing to take some financial risks? There are also many rags-to-riches cases, i.e., many cases of the poor becoming rich and successful through entrepreneurship.

Capitalism works by driving the greed for wealth. The economy could only grow and more jobs could be created only when there are more investments. Who would be so silly to invest their hard-earned money in a risky venture whose chance of success is only normally around say 30% or less, if there isn't much to gain by success? It is thus only those who are greedy for great wealth, even status of being a boss, and not risk averse who would take the plunge into business. The government, as the manager of the capitalist system, would be very happy to encourage this greed for wealth as more and more investments mean more and more jobs created for the people, and more and more tax revenues for the government coffers, and there would be economic success in the country. It is a win-win-win situation.

So the capitalist, or investor, has to have at least one inherent bad quality, viz., greed (for wealth in this case). If there are no such greedy people in the capitalist economy, and if everyone is not greedy and just contented with earning a decent salary as an employee, the capitalist system would fail and everyone would have no job as no investment means no job and no income.

The above explanation shows how greed (for wealth) works to drive the economy.

The only people who would be against the capitalist system are possibly the losers such as the poor, the jobless, and maybe those who are envious of the wealthy.

The possible solution to all this problem of exploitation and abuse in the capitalist system is to ensure capitalists are ethical and professional in their dealings with their workers, their peers and their customers or clients. The government should enforce a code of ethics or code of conduct for the capitalists or bosses to abide by, as well as possibly other regulations to limit excessive greed, e.g., limit the amount of money they could invest per year and/or the number of companies they could set up per year, and/or mandate them to contribute to a workers' welfare fund, etc. The government could also pass a law to turn businesses into social enterprises whereby a percentage of their profits may be channeled to society or charity, e.g., for helping the poor and underprivileged, building schools and hospitals for the people, etc., which would make the capitalists more humane. However, many top political leaders come from businesses, i.e., they own businesses. Would they be willing to pass such regulations which would affect their self-interests? These leaders also might be obligated to businesses, e.g., businesses who have financed their political campaigns, etc., and so might be reluctant or unwilling to pass such regulations affecting businesses.

Fortunately a number of US billionaires have set up foundations to address global problems such as poverty, diseases, climate change, etc., as well as willing the bulk of their vast wealth to charities upon their demise, which is evidence that some of the wealthy capitalists have humanity. There are much problems in capitalism, particularly great disparity in the distribution of wealth and poverty, even famines, hygiene and health problems in the poor countries. The rich capitalists could actually donate funds towards helping these poor countries. Probably a number are already doing it.

Even if there are good, practicable ideas in this chapter, it is probably difficult to have them implemented unless in positions of influence, e.g., as advisors to governments, as the influential economist Keynes had been, or unless somebody of influence likes the ideas and chooses to implement them. At least the ideas are thrown open in public for awareness, debate, refinement and hopefully, at least for some of them, acceptance and implementation for the good of society. As everyone knows economics is not an exact science and is, as someone wittily put it, common sense made difficult for academic study, e.g., in the universities. Thus many of the ideas might look good but might be hard to implement, and if implemented might not bring the expected result. Of course some form of action should be carried out to right any wrongs in the economy and thereby society, especially by the government.

Those who desire changes to the economic system might write articles and books about changing it for the better. This is however talk only but no action. Action should speak louder than words. In the past, the author had wanted to set up a few social enterprises to provide jobs for the unemployed, whose profits would all be donated to charity. He had approached a wealthy businessman, who is a friend, to provide financial support for this project. The businessman was not keen and instead asked the author to help him set up a religious organisation and help manage the organisation by being a member of its management committee which the author was not keen. Without money there is practically nothing anyone could do to help society. Money is apparently power. We might think we could do something for society by writing articles and books and participating in forums, which is probably an illusion. This method would probably work only if the articles and books are well-cited, i.e., influential. The consolation, perhaps also an illusion, is that at least we tried to do something, which may make our conscience feel better, which is probably better than doing nothing, which may make our conscience feel uneasy.

Capitalists not only exploit workers, out of greed for more and more profits, they frequently over-charge customers, short-change customers, even stealthily smuggle in goods to sell without paying the import duties to the government, under-declare their profits to the government to pay less or no taxes, cheat banks through loan scams, and so on. Many of them are not only greedy but are calculative and cunning as well. Unfortunately, consumers can't do without them, for their goods and services are needed, e.g., food, clothes, essential drugs for diseases, etc.

Also, many of the top political leaders are apparently on the side of the capitalists, being from the same social class. So it is difficult to lobby or influence the political leaders to change the capitalist system for the better.

In the economic system, consumers buy at the lowest possible price to save money and sellers sell at the highest possible price to maximise profits. This is a conflict of interests. Workers also sell their labour at the highest possible price and employers also employ workers at the lowest possible price to save money and maximise profits. This is also a conflict of interests.

Thus, as Marx pointed out, there is always a conflict between workers and employers, who would of course pay workers as little as possible to maximise profits. So workers complain about exploitation by their capitalist bosses. Just a thought to possibly solving this worker-capitalist problem. How about making the workers co-capitalists, whereby they share the same aims and objectives as their capitalist bosses? For example, by implementing the following system of remuneration to workers based on profit-sharing and not monthly salaries or daily rates whichever the case may be: Workers are paid their shares of the profits monthly, or even quarterly giving accounts department time to compute profits and shares of profits, e.g., based on a percentage of the profits to be paid to the co-capitalist or worker. The co-capitalist or worker and the capitalist could sign a contract for half year, one year or longer whose earlier termination would incur penalties to either party. If the company loses money neither the co-capitalist nor the capitalist gets any income (with the capitalist bearing the loss as he is the rightful owner of the company). If the company makes money both parties earn their shares of the profits. If the company makes a lot of profits both parties could become rich. This is a variation of the system wherein employees are given shares by their company. Now the worker or co-capitalist has to think like a capitalist to ensure his company survives and makes a lot of profits. The co-capitalists or workers should be given some decision-making powers, with the main capitalist/company owner being the final decision-maker since he officially owns the company. The co-capitalists might fear that the capitalist cheats on their shares of the company's profits. This could possibly be overcome through getting an outside, third party accounting firm to administer the scheme, perhaps the company's outside, third party accounts auditing company. It should be a win-win situation as the capitalist does not pay the co-capitalist or worker anything if the company makes losses (reduced risk due to not having to pay workers salaries when the company is not doing well and making losses). The worker or co-capitalist has to try hard to make sure the company makes a lot of profits, i.e., he would be very highly motivated to work hard and perform well, and wouldn't feel being exploited and might feel proud of being "one of the bosses in the company". There is a catch here - the co-capitalist or worker has to make sure he joins a profitable company and not a loss-making one. Another question is whether the capitalist is willing to dilute his control of the company by adopting this radical scheme - it would probably take a much enlightened capitalist to be able to adopt such a scheme.

This is indeed a radical scheme which might be considered unpractical, but could be considered for reducing or eliminating the long-lasting conflict or class struggle between workers and capitalists. Real estate and insurance agents, who are considered self-employed, normally do not get salaries at all and are paid strictly on commissions and might earn zero income for months. This radical scheme might be better as the worker should be able to earn at least some income to survive. The stumbling-block for this scheme is apparently the capitalist who would probably not be keen to dilute his control of his company; he needs to be an enlightened person to be able to accept the scheme. Any way, as capitalists tend to be greedy, they would rather keep all the profits to themselves than share with the workers. Also, they are not likely to share power with the workers.

People who don't like to see injustices in society might point out the failings of the capitalist system and might vent their unhappiness about the injustices at forums and other platforms. But the capitalists, together with the leaders who lead the democracies, would simply carry on as per normal. It requires luck to find an enlightened, fair-minded leader who would be willing to really do something about these injustices. In the electoral system of government, leaders also have to look after the interests of the common man to secure their votes in the elections. These leaders could also be lobbied to do something about these injustices.

By the way things look, the capitalists have already entrenched themselves in society and even the socialists have joined them now. We have to understand that capitalism promises many good things in life, such as the many kinds of luxuries people are enjoying now, whereas in the socialist societies of the Lenin, Stalin and Mao Tse-tung eras the people had been living a relatively simple, quiet and boring life without any of the capitalist luxuries. There is hardly any chance to change capitalism for the better now and even if someone initiates a revolution to try to change it likely no one would follow him and people might think he is crazy.

Armed revolutions had taken place in the days of feudalism before democracy exists. People living in democracies nowadays have no way or even inclination (because they could always exercise their democratic right to throw out a government not in their favour at the elections, while overthrowing a powerful and tyrannical emperor in the feudal society would have to be carried out by force only as there was no other way to do so, e.g., peacefully by election or voting) to carry out armed revolts except for holding demonstrations, rioting or in more extreme cases acts of terrorism. But such small scale "fighting" could never overthrow a government. Only if a person commands an army, e.g., as a powerful general, could he have a chance of overthrowing the government and bringing about the change he wants. But there had been emperors, e.g., in China, who had overthrown tyrannical emperors and became tyrannical or more tyrannical themselves after becoming emperors.

What is seen as failure and unacceptable in society, which is subjective, might not be deemed so by the majority in society. So in a democracy, the majority who vote for a certain position or leader representing that position would triumph over the minority. Is it right, fair, logical or ethical for the minority to use force or revolution to force the majority to follow them? A person holding the minority view might succeed in persuading the majority to follow him, after which the majority might faithfully and loyally follow him. But force is likely to bring reluctant and unhappy followers and possible rebellion in future. Even if it is a peaceful revolution, such as in the form of presenting contrarian ideas, e.g., by debate, if one tries to overthrow capitalism the powers-that-be wouldn't give one that access at all and one could only argue one's case in some small forum whose effectiveness is doubtful.

The lack of basic necessities such as drinkable water and food resulting in famines happens in the undeveloped or underdeveloped countries, while those in the more developed economies have a number of luxuries; even participating in a forum, e.g., an internet forum, might be considered a luxury for if the person is hungry because he is poor and has no money to buy food, he wouldn't have internet access or the mood to participate in the internet forum, for it is likely he wouldn't have a computer because he has no money to get one.

In every country there are always poor, jobless, income-less and homeless people, developed or underdeveloped countries, only different in degrees.

Democracy might appear like feudalism in disguise, controlled by the capitalist elite, who with their wealth could find ways to manipulate the voters to keep themselves in power, e.g., even paying voters to vote for them, while the poor could not even afford the financial deposits required to stand for elections.

Should we judge democracy harshly? If there are many criminals and crooks in capitalism, socialism, autocracy, etc., could they just alone on this criterion be judged bad? If a person has many good qualities but he has maybe one or two bad qualities, could he be judged bad? Is perfection to be expected?

Meritocracy has been an aspect of democracy, unlike in the feudal past whereby the children of the feudal lords inherited their fathers' high, powerful positions. In democracies nowadays high positions are normally obtained by those with high academic qualifications, e.g., those with MBAs, etc. Hence the paper chase and scramble for top exam grades and elite universities. Again the wealthy capitalist class could afford expensive tuition and coaching for their children and so they again entrench themselves in the academic world.

Much as the capitalists are disdained for their excessive greed, many of them have also set up and funded universities, and awarded scholarships to worthy students, etc. Perhaps many of us are also holding degrees awarded by universities set up and funded by wealthy capitalists. Even the computer we are using now and the social media and internet access, e.g., Facebook, Google, etc., are the inventions and products of capitalists, which people have also been seemingly ungratefully been using to criticise and attack the capitalists, appearing like attacking the hand which has fed them.

Greed for wealth might also be viewed as ambition, e.g., acquiring wealth so that they could do good for society, e.g., by setting up orphanages, hospitals, universities, social enterprises, etc., not dissimilar to a person aiming for higher and higher academic qualifications so that he could obtain a higher post and a higher salary.

To reduce the ill effects of capitalism might be difficult. Many are just happy with whatever luxuries they have and the freedom given under democracy and the linked capitalism. There is possibly a number of people who couldn't stand the injustices and ill effects of capitalism. There are perhaps several ways for this group to express their unhappiness to the authorities, such as writing letters in the forum pages of the newspapers about their concerns whereby the authorities or the government normally would have to reply, joining government committees which debate certain issues, giving feedback to the government through their feedback/service quality control units, forming certain interest groups, e.g., associations or societies, with like-minded people to lobby the government, getting involved in politics, e.g., standing for election for membership of parliament or congress whereby they could debate issues to their hearts' content and where they could really help to change the laws, etc. Forums, e.g., academic ones, are probably more for academics who would like to debate and exchange ideas so that they may produce some papers for publication in research journals.

Papers or books written by academics which have many citations and are influencial could make the authorities notice and the authorities might adopt some or all of these academics' ideas, e.g., in the case of Keynes, etc. Thus writing papers, pamphlets and books might be another way to influence the government. For instance, Keynes, who had served in the British treasury, wrote a famous book criticising government policies "The Economic Consequences of the Peace" (after resigning from the treasury due to some disagreement with its policies). This book was very popular and Keynes became very famous because of this book, having become in effect a public intellectual.

Though there are complaints about capitalism, which could of course never be perfect, a number of socialist countries which embraced capitalism, e.g., China, have been seeing an increase in their standard of living, and their people are enjoying better health and living longer lives. The experts also forecast that with capitalism they expect world poverty to be eradicated by 2030 or so.

Capitalism is a long tested and proven system and relatively few people have serious complaints against it, though it is apparently not a totally fair or just system. It is not going to be easy to replace capitalism when the majority is apparently in favour of it and supports it, i.e., capitalism is already entrenched in society. Otherwise, many people would be overtly objecting to capitalism. The problem is in selecting a more suitable and desirable economic system, which has not been tested and is therefore risky, to replace capitalism.

It could be said that capitalism should benefit the capitalists more than the workers, for capitalists take great risks (much greater than that of workers), for if they are in debt and go bankrupt they would have negative wealth - worse than the poor who have zero wealth. But if their business succeeds they would have wealth and prestige. It could also be said that the worker needs the capitalist (to provide him a job and income) more than the capitalist needs him (to provide the productive labour), now that the worker could be easily replaced by robots and automation. However this point is subjective and arguable.

There might be some who complain that few benefit from capitalism and blame the capitalists for getting most of the benefits out of capitalism. The benefits of capitalism are hard to gauge and are subjective. How does one gauge and be certain that only a few benefit from capitalism while the rest do not which is unfair? It would be self-contradictory of someone to complain that capitalism benefits few people while he is evidently now enjoying and benefiting from capitalism such as enjoying the things and goods produced by capitalists, even possibly depending on the capitalists for employment and income, etc. We cannot say capitalism is no good and yet support it in many ways, e.g., using the products/services manufactured/supplied by capitalists, accepting scholarships awarded by capitalists, studying at the universities set up and supported by capitalists, e.g., MIT, Harvard, etc., which would be self-contradictory, though this implies capitalists still have an essential role in the economy but we have no choice but to depend on the capitalists in this instance as we need their products and services for survival. How could the unfairness of capitalism be rectified?

It is apparent that the capitalists have their selfish interests uppermost, such as profit maximisation and exploitation to maximise profits (which is natural human tendency, viz., greed, ambition, etc.) and would do everything within their power to secure their interests in the economy, e.g., by buying over politicians to support their interests by financially supporting their election campaigns and others, etc. Capitalists would try to exploit every situation to maximise their profits, wealth and power, much as politicians, and autocrats, etc., would. To right the wrongs of capitalism, positive action such as writing to the relevant press forums (with probably many millions of readers) and government agencies, lobbying, politicking, etc., which are legitimate procedures, could probably help.

There has been the trend of professionals, e.g., scientists, researchers, etc., migrating from the socialist countries like Russia, China, Poland, etc., to the western capitalist countries while people from the western capitalist countries migrating to these socialist countries have been hardly heard of. Also, a number of dissenters from the socialist countries, e.g., Russia, China, etc., had been hounded by their autocratic governments till they had to flee to the western capitalist countries for exile and protection, these western capitalist countries apparently being beacons of democracy, freedom of speech and liberty. Though democracy, freedom of speech and liberty are welcome by practically everyone, too much of them would probably result in problems; some of these western capitalist countries, e.g., the US, appear to be too liberal resulting in a delinquency and drug culture.

In cessionalism, an economic system proposed by an European economist, every citizen could be given capital by the government to do business (be a capitalist) but of course not everyone will succeed. Cessionalism, which is another form of capitalism sponsored by the government, which provides free capital to its citizens for investing in businesses wherein at the moment those born into wealthy families have the means to start businesses, could be considered for adoption as a new economic system to replace the existing form of capitalism, as those not from wealthy families could now also start businesses thus giving everyone a fair chance to be an entrepreneur. However, the setback apparently is that if everyone becomes a capitalist or boss in society there wouldn't be anyone left to be workers, who are needed for providing the productive labour, e.g., for the factories, until some of these capitalists fail in their business and look for work.

Capitalism is about investing capital/money to do business and earn profits, which is itself not bad for people have to trade/barter to survive since maybe the cave-men's time. What is bad about capitalism is exploitation/cheating/bullying of workers by their capitalist bosses. However there are also good capitalist bosses who have welfare for workers, perhaps not much. There are workers' unions to fight for the workers and government legislation also protects the workers. So workers are also protected from exploitation if they are unionised and may not be in such bad shape.

Those who oppose capitalism may equate capitalism (doing business) with exploitation (cheating). There are however business people who treat their workers well, who are happy working for them. To protect workers' basic rights practically all governments have acts, e.g., the Employment Act, to ensure workers are not unfairly treated by employers and given basic rights, eg., off-days, medical leave, annual leave, overtime pay, etc. Employment Acts normally protect workers only but not executive, managerial and secretarial staff. If one claims capitalists are a scourge in society due to their greed and exploitation, there are also capitalists running social enterprises for the good of society. Under the government legislations, employers normally have the right to hire, fire and retrench staff, but they have to follow the governmental/legally prescribed procedures and ensure their fired/retrenched workers are not fired due to victimisation and are fairly/properly compensated. Under such circumstances, governments are in effect curbing exploitation by capitalists. As all businesses apparently only care about profits and are answerable to their shareholders and boards of directors on profitability, companies have little hesitation in retrenching workers due to poor business, which might seem ruthless. Unions might be there to protect workers from being unfairly treated and unfairly terminated by their employers. But union leaders could be bought over by management, though these might be exceptions, and they might not really protect workers.

One should not mix up doing business with exploitation of workers. Business men clearly want to make money but have to serve the needs of their customers to earn their money. They advertise and have sales gimmicks to attract customers. One cannot assume workers are weak and stupid and employers can easily exploit and cheat them. In fact workers are often shrewd and calculative. If the capitalists offer low salaries, poor benefits, no promotion prospects, and no or little welfare, etc., one could be assured that no workers would join their companies. Workers would compare the salaries and benefits of various companies and join those companies who pay them better wages, benefits, etc. Even after joining a company they would frequently resign if unhappy. There is apparently hardly any question of exploitation. The labour market is a free market and wages, benefits, etc., are determined by market forces such as demand and supply of labour. A number of investors have moved out of countries whose labour costs are too high and whose workers are too demanding and choosy about jobs, e.g., move to China where labour has been plentiful and cheap. If workers were willing to join a company and accept the company's low salaries and benefits, it is not the company's fault as the company did not force or order the workers to join their company - the workers willingly join their company. In fact the company does not owe the workers a living. Many companies also offer high salaries and good benefits to attract workers. This is hardly exploitation.

Job-hopping (workers joining another company for a pay increase, etc.) has been such a serious problem that bosses at one time complained a lot about such seemingly irresponsible and unprofessional behaviour of the job-hopping workers and some governments had to step in to stop this trend of endemic job-hopping which causes disruption to the economy.

Those who oppose capitalism might say that the wealth of the capitalists are due to the labour of their workers and the workers should have a share of their wealth. Is this logical? The capitalists bought the labour of the workers with money (wages) - this is bartering/trading of labour for money between capitalist and worker. Besides, the workers do not own the company. Workers can have a share of the wealth if they own part of the company, e.g., have shares or partnership in the company as has quite often happened. Any way capitalists do give bonuses to their workers. On the other hand, if the company makes losses or goes bankrupt, should the workers also share in the losses, e.g., by having pay cuts, forgoing their salaries or also facing bankruptcy proceedings, besides sharing profits in good times? For instance, if a person paid some workers to build his house and later the workers tell him that since they contributed to his house through their hard work and insist on living in his house and/or having a share of the sales proceeds of the house when he sells his house, should the person give in to the workers' "reasoned" request? If, e.g., a government leader considers all capitalists undesirable and orders all the capitalists to close shop or move out of the country, what would happen? Suddenly everyone is jobless and without income. There is no one to supply goods and services, e.g., food, medical products and services, etc. Unless the government is prepared to take over all the industries and businesses as in socialism, there would be deep trouble.

Management books all teach Maslow's Hierarchy of Needs (human needs) and how to motivate workers and increase their productivity. Thus companies should not maximise their profits by treating their workers like cows, pigs and horses and drive them like crazy to work very hard.

Many workers also later become capitalists and since they have this prospect workers would not be so silly as to be against capitalism. If producing, selling things and trading in capitalism are bad and undesirable, what other things can people do for a living? Everyone has to sell or trade something with others to survive, e.g., a product or a service to a customer or customers, one's labour to a capitalist in exchange for money (wages), and so on.

A number of people may favour socialism as the preferred economic system over capitalism, whereby all industries and businesses are owned and controlled by the government, by and for the people of the country, which is evidently a very fair economic system wherein there would be more equality. Socialist countries, e.g., Russia and China, which had abandoned capitalism under the feudal system and turned to socialism, may have made a mistake by now going back to capitalism wherein social ills like corruption, and even exploitation of workers, have apparently returned.

Probably an economic system comprising of the best, most desirable elements of both capitalism and socialism would be ideal. Socialist countries like Russia and China have lately introduced capitalism in their countries and in China, e.g., due to private ownership of businesses now (capitalism), the standard of living of the people has increased and the Chinese are enjoying better health and living longer lives. The Chinese apparently could succeed very well in business in China because they are business-minded, risk-takers and have drive. Many Chinese are also successful in business in other countries they migrated to, e.g., in the US, Canada, Australia, etc.

Though capitalism might be regarded by some as a scourge to society by turning people into modern slaves, etc., there could possibly come a time when due to robots, automation and AI displacing human labour and causing mass unemployment, loss of income and livelihood, the people would revolt against the government, the capitalists and their related kind, following the example of the Luddites who had destroyed the equipment which had displaced them during the industrial revolution; the people would likely revolt if really forced into a corner with no means of survival. Even if capitalism ends, as some might wish it to, a new form of capitalism (neo-capitalism) could arise as people are so creative.

It may be thought desirable for governments to provide some financial aid for the unemployed so that they may be able to at least start some small businesses. Though there are countries providing unemployment benefits for the jobless a number of countries refrain from doing so because if the jobless receive unemployment benefits they may not be keen to look for work.

Maybe all business organisations should be social enterprises, whereby all or a percentage of their profits are channeled to society and charity. This is another economic idea to consider.

An economic system should see to it that everyone has a decent job with a decent income, that there is little or no poverty, and that there is mutual respect between workers and employers and little or no exploitation of workers. This should be somewhat the ideal to aim for.

12

Covid-19 Pandemic, the Economy and Possible Remedies

Covid-19 has made its unexpected entrance into the world some time in late 2019 causing much fear, economic disasters, suffering and fatalities throughout the world.

When Covid-19 first appeared the World Health Organization (WHO) had advised that the virus spread through physical contact and not through the air and thus wearing face masks was not necessary unless one was not well. How wrong could the WHO be when it was later discovered that the virus also spreads contagiously by air, making the wearing of face masks for preventing the contagious spread of the virus more or less a necessity. Sad to say there are many delusory people who prefer to view Covid-19 as similar to the common flu and should be regarded as nothing more serious than the common flu, whereby they end up paying a heavy price by falling seriously ill, or even die, due to the virus.

Many countries have relaxed and let their guard down resulting in second, third or more waves of the infection. As the virus seems adamant to stay and refuses to go away, Covid-19 would become endemic, a new normal, similar to the common flu, dengue, and what have you.

Over-crowding also appears to cause the virus to spread quickly and easily. As we are all social beings, gathering in groups is desirable but this would help to hasten the spread of the virus. In this respect, the virus has put a damper on social interaction and gatherings. People can't go to the office and work because they might catch or spread the virus in groups there and have to work from home, they can't gather in big social groups such as parties and weddings, they can't travel freely for fear of catching or spreading the virus, students can't physically attend class on many days and have to take lessons via the internet, and so on. Because travel is not allowed, the tourist industry is badly hit and the related supporting service companies such foreign currency exchange and souvenirs supply companies are also badly affected. In short, economic activities are adversely affected and quite a number of companies have retrenched staff or have closed for good. Humanity appears to be losing to the virus in many ways.

The elderly, and even the very young, whose immune systems tend to be weak, are particularly vulnerable to infection by the virus, and, if infected it could be fatal for them.

Some possible measures for curbing Covid-19 are suggested. Humanity should not allow themselves to be sitting ducks waiting for the virus to attack, seeing how aggressively the virus has been contagiously attacking them; they should find ways to counter-attack the virus, and stop it from infecting them. In fact, to admit that Covid-19 would be endemic and would be the new normal is to admit defeat by the virus.

Many countries are getting their people, especially the elderly and vulnerable, vaccinated against infection, if possible the whole population, so that there would be herd immunity, so that the various restrictions imposed to stop the spread of the virus could be eased and life could return to normal. But there are many problems in this move, for example, not enough doses of the vaccine to go round, people who refuse to be vaccinated due to lack of confidence in the vaccines, fear of side effects, infection even after partial or full vaccination, re-infection, etc.

For hotter climates, for example, in countries such as Thailand, Vietnam, Africa, etc., which have tropical or sub-tropical climates, Covid-19 infections and casualties are relatively much lower than those in the colder countries, for example, US, UK, Canada, France, Italy, Iran, Sweden, etc. It has been found that the hotness of the tropical and sub-tropical countries puts a damper on or kill the viruses while the cold of the colder countries encourages their survival and proliferation.

The following measures, on top of the other measures in use, are suggested for curbing Covid-19:-

(1) "Heating" equipment for reducing or eliminating infection by inactivating or killing the virus might be more practical for colder countries, especially in winters, besides keeping people warm. As the viruses could not survive at high temperatures, "high temperature generating" equipment, for example, hot-air blowers for both indoor and outdoor, might be viable for use against the virus. Evidently, the viruses could not withstand heat. A recent experiment in a French lab found that the viruses became inactive when the temperature was high; but the viruses died only when the temperature was near boiling point. This might explain why tropical or sub-tropical countries such as Vietnam, Thailand, Burma and Africa have relatively much less Covid-19 infections and casualties than colder countries such as US, UK, Canada and France.

(2) Covid-19 is now confirmed also an air-borne disease. This means staying indoors may not be safe. For example, a gust of wind carrying the viruses blowing into the house or anywhere in the environment may infect people with the viruses. Vaccines provide the cure. Prevention is evidently better than cure. For prevention, there are disinfectants and UV lights which kill the virus, detergents, face-masks, face-shields, etc. However, it would probably be better to have air-filtering equipment, for both indoor and outdoor, which suck in air, filter away the viruses and other harmful substances from the air and release virus-free, clean air into the environment. Someone, who is probably an inventor, has been heard saying that he is attempting to make such an equipment, and, this is certainly a good preventive method. This would possibly be the most effective way of fighting Covid-19 if the equipment were available. Such air-filtering equipment might also be suitable for simultaneously filtering away other types of air-borne viruses and bacteria, for example, those that cause influenza, pneumonia and tuberculosis, which would be "killing more than one bird with one stone".

(3) The idea here might seem far-fetched but it might work. It is said that there are plenty of "good" and "bad" bacteria in the human body, for example, in the guts; the "good" bacteria in the body fight the "bad" bacteria and prevent the latter from causing harm to the body. Likewise, it might be possible to have "good" viruses or bacteria to fight and neutralize Covid-19, inside and outside the human body.

Developing the equipment and carrying out the micro-biological research suggested in the above-mentioned methods may require a lot of funding, e.g., from the government, as well as technical expertise.

Vaccines might not be effective especially if the virus could mutate or change very quickly and become resistant to them quickly, now that they are available, which probably explains why there are fully vaccinated people who still get infected by the virus. Though vaccines are important for the cure and vaccinated people would not fall so ill if infected by the virus, prevention from infection should take precedence as infection might cause serious problems such as multiple organs failure if not death and a weakened body even if the person recovers.

The three suggested, possible ways of curbing the spread of the virus presented above should be seriously considered. While the important measures such as vaccination are defensive, these three suggested, possible methods are aggressive, offensive and preventive. Prevention is evidently better than cure.

Another concern is that face masks are not fool-proof against the virus. When a person breathes through the mask, unfiltered air also gets breathed in from the sides of the face mask. Air is fluid and it travels in all directions. The virus through transmission by air could land on any part of the person's body, in fact anywhere.

Many people are infected by Covid-19 and dying every day. Vaccinations and masks, though important, are only defensive weapons against the virus. They do not attack and eradicate the enemy, which is the virus, allowing it to continue causing trouble. More aggressive and offensive methods should be used, such as the three methods suggested above, in order to eradicate or get rid of the virus which is causing much harm and deaths every day, in order to stop the virus from contagiously infecting more people, before it is too late. This may be easier said than done but this, if carried out, could effectively put a damper on Covid-19 infections. However, vaccinations are evidently for strengthening the body against/curing the body from Covid-19 infection only, while the methods suggested above are for preventing Covid-19 infection - there is a world of difference between the two. A more preemptive and preventive measure against the virus should be adopted to stop it from causing further harm and deaths. The best defence against the virus now wherein virus infections are getting more serious in many countries appears to be more aggressive intervention or more offensive action against the virus. The reason also, besides stopping the virus from contagiously infecting more people, is that if the virus is not eradicated and allowed to survive and thrive it could mutate into a stronger, more dangerous, more contagious virus (as has already happened, with there being several new, more contagious strains of the virus), whereby it would become harder, possibly impossible even, to eradicate, with the Covid-19 situation becoming more intractable as a result. In the past, when the bird flu outbreaks occurred, hordes of fowls infected by the bird flu were quickly rounded up and culled, thereby eradicating the bird flu virus and ending the outbreaks. Humanity could not do the same to its own kind. The above-mentioned suggested, possible methods of eradicating the Covid-19 virus possibly represent the next best alternative.

At the moment, the virus appears to be having the upper hand in the "game of chess" with humanity. Whatever steps have been taken to counter the viral infection so far, the virus has apparently been able to counter-block, mutate and become more contagious, causing consternation and fear. Evidently a better strategy is required for containing the virus, as in a game of chess against a chess opponent, or, in a war against the enemy.

In the news, more infections and more deaths are heard every day, and more and more companies, e.g., restaurants and pubs, are closing down, which is worrying; on the other hand, businesses supplying sanitary products such as gloves, face-masks and hand sanitisers, as well as pharmaceutical products and medical services, have boomed, with a number of their proprietors even becoming billionaires. Should this state of affairs be allowed to continue and should the situation be simply treated as endemic and the new normal, that is, should the infections and deaths be treated as normal and be allowed to continue? Should people continue to live in abject fear of the virus? What about counter-measures which could rectify all this? Positive thinkers would say the fight has to continue and the battle has to be won; otherwise it would be doom. Soldiers win battles by advancing and killing their enemies and not by staying put and allowing their enemies to attack; team sports players win matches by charging forward and scoring goals at their opponents' goal-mouth and not by staying put and allowing their opponents to charge at them and score goals at their own goal-mouth. In the battle against the virus the same principle should apply.

It is with hope that the above-mentioned possible elimination of the Covid-19 virus is achieved and economic activities can be back to normal soon, but experts have warned that recovery may take a long time, many years or even decades.

Reading List

[1] The General Theory of Employment, Interest, and Money, John Maynard Keynes, Harcourt, Inc., 1964
[2] Principles of Economics, Paul Samuelson, McGraw Hill, 2010
[3] The Making of Modern Economics, Mark Skousen, Routledge, 2016
[4] Essentials of Economics, John Sloman, Pearson, 2019
[5] The Wealth of Nations, Adam Smith, The Modern Library, 1994

About the Author

The author is a professor who has been teaching business subjects. He has published about 40 books.

www.ingramcontent.com/pod-product-compliance
Lightning Source LLC
Chambersburg PA
CBHW082121220526

45472CB00009B/2267